"*Who Took My Money*' is an esse: habit change and proactive control.

What a remarkable source of inspiration, profoundly influencing people's approach to money management. Through this, I've learned a critical financial lesson: the importance of prioritizing my financial well-being. It's a change that's both empowering and enlightening, offering a fresh perspective on personal finance.

Thank you for all your great financial wisdom, kindness, and compassion over the years! You are an inspiration to us all! Congratulations! I LOVE your new book!"

*Lynda Damen*—Congratulations! I LOVE your new book!
*Director, Homelessness Society of the Bow Valley*
*Chair-Elect, Canmore Rotary Club Community Grants Programs*


"Monique Gagné has a gift for teaching people that saving and investing money can be loads of fun at any age. Stop worrying or feeling guilty about your finances. Start enjoying a brighter future today."

*Steve Harrison*—Co-founder, www.AuthorSuccess.com


"*Who Took My Money?* is an easy-to-read refresher on the basics of saving money and using it wisely. Author Monique and co-author Cathie have created characters, such as the wise grandfather GP, who shares his wisdom with his grandson, Charles, in the family garage. Anyone can grasp the information and, within a few hours of easy reading, will have the knowledge and comprehension of the financial jargon needed to keep and accumulate wealth—simple reminders like Self-Check, Ask Yourself, and inspirations are exactly what the consumer needs. Great job, ladies!"

*Paul Grimes, CLU, CFP, CHFC*
*Senior Vice President IA Financial Group*
*Author of The Facts of Life*

# WHO TOOK MY MONEY?

# WHO TOOK MY MONEY?

**Discover Timeless Secrets of Smart Money Moves to Protect Your Assets**

**Monique Gagné**
Author

**Cathie Orfali**
Co-Author

Copyright © 2024
All rights reserved

**Who Took My Money?**

**Legal Disclaimer**
This publication is designed to provide accurate information regarding the subject matter to instill good financial practices in all our readers. It is sold with the understanding that the publisher does not render legal, accounting, or other professional services. If legal advice or additional expert assistance is required, the services of a competent professional should be sought.

Care has been taken to trace the ownership of copyright material contained in this book; however, the publisher welcomes any information that enables anyone to rectify any reference or credit for subsequent editions.

Our objective is to empower people to take charge of their Money, through our unique and creative approach.

**Author**: Monique Gagné (*Amyot*) – Mortgage Agent / Financial Coach
Co-Author: Cathie Orfali – EPC / CFP / CEA / MFA-P
Design/Layout/Review: Mike Beaudin, Suzanne Fortier-Gour
Illustrations: Camil Gravel, Marc-André Bédard

**Who Took My Money?**
Second edition – new version from the original book 2008 © by Monique Amyot. All rights reserved. The text of this publication, or any part thereof, may not be reproduced in any manner whatsoever without written permission from the author.

Printed in Canada

ISBN (paperback): 978-1-0689492-1-0
ISBN (ebook): 978-1-0689492-2-7

1. Finance, Personal. 2. Financial Security 3. Self-Help

Book design and production by www.AuthorSuccess.com

Trade books are available at special quantity discounts for sales promotions, employee premiums, or educational purposes.

To learn more about ® personal Money management, and financial tools please visit **moniquegagne.com** whotookmymoney.ca / solutionfinance.ca / moneyadvisors.ca

*P.S. In this book, we treat Money with the respect it deserves, even honoring it with a capital "M"—just as we would with a dear friend's name.*

# CONTENTS

FORWORD . . . . . . . . . . . . . . . . . . . . . . . . . . . . . . . . . . . . . . . . . . . . . . . . . . . . . . . . X
INTRODUCTION: THE STORY BEHIND 'WHO TOOK MY MONEY?' . . . . . . . . . . . . . . . . . 1
**CHAPTER 1: WHAT IS MONEY?** . . . . . . . . . . . . . . . . . . . . . . . . . . . . . . . . . . . . . . . 7
    *Managing Money* . . . . . . . . . . . . . . . . . . . . . . . . . . . . . . . . . . . . . . . . . . . . . . 8
    *The Evolution of Money* . . . . . . . . . . . . . . . . . . . . . . . . . . . . . . . . . . . . . . . . 9
    *Time, Benefit, and Money* . . . . . . . . . . . . . . . . . . . . . . . . . . . . . . . . . . . . . . 10
    *Navigating Life with Money as Your Co-Pilot* . . . . . . . . . . . . . . . . . . . . . . . . 11
    *GP's Money Principles* . . . . . . . . . . . . . . . . . . . . . . . . . . . . . . . . . . . . . . . . . 13
**CHAPTER 2: FINANCIAL PITFALLS** . . . . . . . . . . . . . . . . . . . . . . . . . . . . . . . . . . . 15
    *The Shocking State of Personal Finances* . . . . . . . . . . . . . . . . . . . . . . . . . . . 16
    *Money Traps and Pitfalls* . . . . . . . . . . . . . . . . . . . . . . . . . . . . . . . . . . . . . . . 17
    *Hard Lessons: Unveiling the Pitfalls* . . . . . . . . . . . . . . . . . . . . . . . . . . . . . . . 18
    *Fraud: Too Good to Be True, Trust Your Intuition* . . . . . . . . . . . . . . . . . . . . . 18
    *Should You Loan Money to Family Members?* . . . . . . . . . . . . . . . . . . . . . . . 19
    *Scammed Out of a Down Payment:* . . . . . . . . . . . . . . . . . . . . . . . . . . . . . . . 20
    *Get It in Writing!* . . . . . . . . . . . . . . . . . . . . . . . . . . . . . . . . . . . . . . . . . . . . 20
    *The Self-Check!* . . . . . . . . . . . . . . . . . . . . . . . . . . . . . . . . . . . . . . . . . . . . . 22
**CHAPTER 3: MIND OVER MONEY** . . . . . . . . . . . . . . . . . . . . . . . . . . . . . . . . . . . 25
    *The Importance of Self-Talk* . . . . . . . . . . . . . . . . . . . . . . . . . . . . . . . . . . . . 26
    *Tuning up Your Beliefs about Money* . . . . . . . . . . . . . . . . . . . . . . . . . . . . . 27
    *Beliefs Cheat Sheet* . . . . . . . . . . . . . . . . . . . . . . . . . . . . . . . . . . . . . . . . . . 28
    *Commitment to Change* . . . . . . . . . . . . . . . . . . . . . . . . . . . . . . . . . . . . . . . 29
    *Time to Replace Old Beliefs* . . . . . . . . . . . . . . . . . . . . . . . . . . . . . . . . . . . . 29
    *When Dreams Become Reality* . . . . . . . . . . . . . . . . . . . . . . . . . . . . . . . . . . 31
**CHAPTER 4: DARE TO DREAM** . . . . . . . . . . . . . . . . . . . . . . . . . . . . . . . . . . . . . 33
    *Dreams: The Blueprint of Ambition* . . . . . . . . . . . . . . . . . . . . . . . . . . . . . . . 34
    *Setting SMART Goals* . . . . . . . . . . . . . . . . . . . . . . . . . . . . . . . . . . . . . . . . . 35
    *Pursuing Your Dreams* . . . . . . . . . . . . . . . . . . . . . . . . . . . . . . . . . . . . . . . . 36
**CHAPTER 5: THE FINANCIAL TOOL KIT, PART 1** . . . . . . . . . . . . . . . . . . . . . . . . . 39
    *Get Back to Basics* . . . . . . . . . . . . . . . . . . . . . . . . . . . . . . . . . . . . . . . . . . . 39
    *Organizing Your Documents* . . . . . . . . . . . . . . . . . . . . . . . . . . . . . . . . . . . . 40
    *The Snapshot: Your Net Worth Statement* . . . . . . . . . . . . . . . . . . . . . . . . . . 41
    *Let's Play: Cash-Only Spending Challenge* . . . . . . . . . . . . . . . . . . . . . . . . . . 45

## CHAPTER 6: THE FINANCIAL TOOL KIT, PART 2 .... 49
*GP's Healthy Money Cycle* .... 50
*My Budget (sample)* .... 53
*Financial Account Guide* .... 56
*Adjust (Review)* .... 57
*Audit 1–2–3* .... 58

## CHAPTER 7: NEEDS AND WANTS! .... 63
*Decoding Needs and Wants* .... 65
*Learn to Be Frugal* .... 66
*Smart Strategies for Savvy Spending* .... 66
*Big Ticket Cost: The Dream Boat* .... 67
*Dreaming of Open Waters* .... 68
*Buy Out of Season* .... 68
*Buying New versus Buying Used* .... 69

## CHAPTER 8: MODERN CHAINS .... 73
*Credit Danger Signals* .... 74
*GP's Debt Management Guidelines* .... 75
*Debt Consolidation* .... 76
*The Toolbox Tasks: Pay It Off!* .... 77
*Let's Play: A Mini Quiz* .... 78

## CHAPTER 9: YOUR RELATIONSHIP .... 83
*GP's Step-by-Step Guide for Couples* .... 84
*Possessions Can Imprison Us* .... 88
*The Credit Report Journey* .... 88

## CHAPTER 10: A WEALTHY MINDSET .... 91
*What Wealthy People Have in Common* .... 92
*The Rich Mindset* .... 93
*The Illusion of Wealth: Danger Signals* .... 94
*From Rags to Riches* .... 94
*The Financial Habits of Millionaires* .... 95
*Fine-Tuning My Finances* .... 97

## CHAPTER 11: THE GOLDEN RULES .... 99
*The Golden Rule* .... 100
*Why Should You Be the First Payee?* .... 101
*The Power of Compound Growth* .... 101
*The Power of Numbers!* .... 103

## CHAPTER 12: GIVE YOUR MONEY A JOB ... 109
*Investments in Dreamyville* ... 111
*The Pit Stop of Registered Savings Accounts* ... 113
*Multiple Streams of Income Choices* ... 116
*The Tax Collector* ... 117
*Battling Inflation* ... 118
*Shifting Gears to Business Ownership* ... 119
*Transitioning into Emergency Funds* ... 120

## CHAPTER 13: GETTING AHEAD IN REAL ESTATE ... 125
*Navigating the Real Estate Highway* ... 126
*Home Buying Steps: Navigating with Experts* ... 127
*Declaring War on Your Mortgage* ... 128
*Becoming a Savvy Estate Investor* ... 130
*Who Is Your Support System?* ... 130

## CHAPTER 14: PROTECTION FROM THE STORM ... 135
*Who Do You Need to Protect?* ... 136
*Types of Insurance: Your Protection Toolbox* ... 137

## CHAPTER 15: GET THE KIDS INVOLVED ... 143
*Teaching Your Kids About Money* ... 144
*Responsibility to Our Children* ... 144
*Teach by Example* ... 145
*Make It Easy and Fun* ... 146
*Finances 101 in High School* ... 147
*GP's Legacy of Financial Wisdom* ... 148

## CHAPTER 16: TAKING CARE OF SENIORS ... 151
*Retirement and the Senior Milestone* ... 152
*Navigating Post-Retirement Work and Benefits* ... 153
*Fraud Prevention* ... 154
*Cash Management* ... 156
*The True Wealth of Senior Well-Being* ... 156

## CHAPTER 17: LEAVING A LEGACY ... 159
*The Gift of Responsibility* ... 160
*Giving Back to Charity* ... 160
*Where Does My Money Go When I Die?* ... 161
*Dying Without a Will (Intestate)* ... 163
*How to Write a Will* ... 164

**YOUR 30-DAY CHALLENGE** .................................................... 168
   *To Kick-Start Your Financial Journey* ............................................... 168
   *My Financial Well-Being* .......................................................... 169
   *Keeping a Financial Journal* ...................................................... 169
   *Involving the Family in Finances* .................................................. 170
   *30-Day Financial Transformation Plan*............................................. 171
   *Week 1: Establishing a Strong Foundation* ......................................... 171
   *Week 2: Building Awareness and Making Adjustments* ............................. 172
   *Week 3: Gaining Control and Protecting Assets*..................................... 172
   *Week 4: Reinforcing Good Habits and Celebrating Progress* ........................ 172
   *Ongoing Commitment* ........................................................... 172
   *Embracing the Financial Journey* .................................................. 173

**GP'S EASY TIPS FOR FINANCIAL MANAGEMENT**.............................174
   *Reflections on Wealth and Life*..................................................... 175

**ADDITIONAL READING**.....................................................177
**BIBLIOGRAPHY** ............................................................178
**RESOURCES** ...............................................................179
**DEAR READER** .............................................................180
**UNDERSTANDING FINANCIAL TERMS**........................................181
**ACKNOWLEDGMENTS**......................................................183
**MONIQUE GAGNÉ, MONEY-MOM**...........................................184
**CATHIE ORFALI, EPC, CFP, CEA, MFA-P** .......................................185

# FOREWORD

Dear Readers,

It is with genuine excitement that I introduce you to Monique Gagné's and Cathie Orfali's remarkable book, *Who Took My Money?* Within the pages that follow, they generously share their practical wisdom and actionable strategies, empowering you on your unique financial journey. Whether you're a student, recent graduate embarking on your professional life or someone seeking to enhance your financial literacy, this book holds valuable insights that resonate.

**WHY THIS BOOK MATTERS**

Monique and Cathie approach personal finance with both clarity and empathy. Here are some compelling reasons why you should eagerly delve into *Who Took My Money?*:

Financial Foundations: They demystify complex financial concepts, acting as your trusted guide through budgeting, debt management, and investing. Consider them your personal coach, helping you construct a solid financial groundwork.

Mindset Shifts: Beyond mere numbers, they emphasize the power of mindset. They encourage you to view money not as an abstract figure, but as a dynamic tool for achieving your life goals. Prepare to shift from financial stress to empowerment.

Practical Exercises: They provide practical, actionable exercises throughout the book. They're like gym workouts for your wallet. Roll up your sleeves and apply what you learn—it's where true transformation happens.

## YOUR JOURNEY BEGINS

As you embark on this enlightening journey:

Read & Reflect: Take the time to immerse yourself in Monique's and Cathie's words. Their insights act as compass points, guiding you toward financial clarity.

Practice Patience: Financial mastery isn't an overnight feat. Their exercises are akin to reps at the financial gym. Consistency matters, and celebrating small wins accumulates into significant progress.

Share the Knowledge: Imagine a world where everyone understands compound interest and makes informed financial decisions. Once you've benefited from Monique's and Cathie's wisdom, pay it forward.

Remember, this book isn't merely about dollars—it's about dreams. So turn those pages, underline key passages, and allow them to be your trusted financial mentor.

May your financial journey be both rewarding and enriching as you build your personal wealth and wisdom.

Elaine Taylor
President, Mortgage Alliance.

INTRODUCTION

# THE STORY BEHIND WHO TOOK MY MONEY?

**There are two primary choices in life: to accept conditions as they exist or accept the responsibility for changing them.**
—DENIS WAITLEY

I was washing the dishes when the loud ring of the phone shattered the calm of our kitchen. Mom answered, and her expression immediately shifted—a sign of trouble. "We need to go to the hospital. It's your dad," she said with urgency. Dad was severely injured, and his survival through the night was uncertain.

Mom's worried eyes met mine. We were five siblings, ranging from three to eleven years old, dependent on our parents. Dad earned a living from his garage, while Mom nurtured us at home. But now, with Dad hospitalized, pressing questions loomed: How would we manage the medical expenses, food, and bills?

Thankfully, my parents had always been careful, like squirrels storing away dollars, investing to secure our future. From their lifestyle and wise savings, our house was paid off, with no loans or debts. But the savings my parents had weren't going to be enough to handle this emergency. My mother tried to get a bank loan, but she was declined due to no income. She then attempted to get government help but was ineligible because our home was owned outright. It was my father's older brother who took over managing my father's company in his absence and this got us through those scary times without falling apart; our family remained intact, avoiding financial ruin. My father recovered, his health restored through the collective effort and support of our family and his brother's stewardship. Life, once disrupted, found its rhythm again as he returned home. As I reflect back now, washing dishes in the very kitchen where the phone once rang with grim news, I realize how resilience and love steered us back to days where happiness and health prevail.

Then, at age forty, I endured a challenging chapter in my life, misguided by the wrong company which led to financial decisions resulting in the end of my long-standing marriage. With twenty-five years turned to memory and little to my name, I started anew. Poor choices led to a financial depression, unsure of how I would survive. What rescued me was my commitment to non-stop work and spending only on necessities. Within a decade years, I had regained my financial freedom, mental well-being, and became the owner of a house and had a successful business as a financial coach and top-performing mortgage agent. The harsh lessons from my experiences, coupled with my parents' wise teachings, empowered me to guide thousands out of debt and steer clear of fiscal pitfalls. Hence, my nickname: Money-Mom. I now enjoy a worry-free lifestyle with real estate in my portfolio, no debt, and the capacity to give back.

My father always said, "Understanding money is the tricky part." He fixed cars, but he also mastered the mechanics of financial peace. His advice—now encapsulated in this book and my course, "The Power of Financial Happiness"—continues to enlighten many.

Even after fifteen years since the release of the first version, people continue to struggle with managing Money. In this updated version of my 2008 book, I asked my colleague Cathie to team up as my co-author. Her commitment and numerous accreditations add great value to the book. Cathie recognizes that monetary achievement is only meaningful when it translates into a life of significance.

Through these pages, we continue the journey we began in season one, where we met Charles at the age of 17, learning the ropes of finance and working by his grandfather's side, mastering both the mechanics of cars and finance. Charles, still in finance, has now advanced to become the director in the Northern region, focusing on agriculture and renowned for producing top-quality maple syrup.

Now, as the story continues, envision sitting in a cozy garage, a warm conversation between my father, known as GP, and my son Charles as they unravel economic truths. Get ready for a read that might change your financial outlook. After all, life's most insightful talks often take place where you least expect them.

> **People only accept change when faced with necessity, and only recognize necessity when a crisis is upon them.**
> —Jean Monnet

For some time, you might have been wondering how to manage your finances efficiently or how to assist a loved one with theirs.

Money management skills aren't something we are born with. The proof is out! Looking at the economy today, it is obvious that we have been doing it wrong. Is it because we find it boring or, taboo to talk about Money, or simply a lack of discipline?

Our life's purpose isn't just about acquiring wealth; it's about ensuring that Money actively works for us to achieve our dreams and happiness.

Now, let's address the burning question: WHO TOOK YOUR MONEY!

### Change your habits:

- A poor mindset is a choice: spending before earning leads to overdrafts.
- A wealthy mindset is also a choice: earn first, then spend wisely.
- Taking control of your finances is your choice.

### Cultivate positive beliefs about Money:

- Believe that you are worthy of it.
- Affirm that you will have as much Money as your heart desires.

### Respect Money:

- Take care of your Money, and it will take care of you.
- Create a financial plan that brings joy and purpose to your life.

The choices you make, your mindset, and how well you're willing to care for your Money—will all determine your financial outcomes. You are the driver of your financial vehicle; decide when to hit the brakes, steer clear of financial pitfalls, and cruise down the financial highway. Taking charge and shifting your mindset will drive you toward the financial future that you envision.

You hold the keys to clarity, commitment, and decision-making. Managing Money should be an engaging, rich with insights and rewards.

**ASK YOURSELF:**

- What do I want most in life –REALLY?
- What keeps me from achieving the life I want for myself and my loved ones?
- What legacy do I wish to leave behind when I die?
- Whether you aspire to wealth or a simple life of fulfilment, finding happiness is paramount.
- As we embark on this financial journey, clarity in your objectives is crucial to finding out who took your Money.

Rev up your engines . . .

    your grand financial expedition awaits.

## A LITTLE INSPIRATION
### MONEY the Magical Wonderer

In the heart of the little village of Prosper, stories tell of a peculiar creature named MONEY. It resembled a green alien with big eyes and sensitive ears that could discern the subtlest financial discrepancies. Most viewed him with suspicion, considering his wild nature. Yet, unknown to many, he harbored deep secrets: MONEY was the greatest financial mechanic, a master at holding cash for wants.

Brin, whose dreams were as vast as the cosmos, saw beyond MONEY's unusual façade. Believing in MONEY's potential, he sought friendship, offering nurture and respect.

Their early days were like trying to align the gears of an old clock, occasionally missing their synchrony. Despite his expertise, MONEY was still drawn to the siren songs of risky ventures. But Brin's patience and wisdom set a steady rhythm between them.

Over time, as Brin nourished their relationship, MONEY revealed his true nature. The green alien became a loyal friend and the mastermind behind Brin's financial success, weaving intricate financial solutions like no other.

In Prosper, tales of their legendary partnership echoed. Brin and MONEY embodied a lesson: the wildest beings can become allies and true friends for life with understanding and patience.

CHAPTER 1

# WHAT IS MONEY?

"Money is neither my god nor my devil. It is a form of energy that tends to make us more of who we already are, whether it's greedy or loving."
—DAN MILLMAN

Money is a valuable tool. Imagine it as a seed you plant that grows into a tree of wealth. It's like being a wise player in a game of chess, strategically planning each move.

GP reflected on all the stress people and their families experience around financial issues. He shared a simple yet profound truth with his grandson: "The mechanic of finance shouldn't cause you stress—but rather—mirror how your perception, knowledge, and values align with its fundamental principle. One must understand the value of Money and apply the law of attraction."

**ASK YOURSELF:**

- What does Money mean to me?
- What do I truly envision for my financial future?
- Do I believe that Money is a fix-all?
- Do I really care for my Money honestly?

Charles and GP tinkered with an old car, nearing the final stages of the repair. With GP wiping his hands on a rag, he turned to Charles. This was the perfect moment to shift gears and delve into the mechanics of financial management.

**MANAGING MONEY**

Charles: "GP, tell me, if managing Money is easy, why do so many struggle with it?

GP: "The simplicity of Money management is deceptive. It's not just about numbers; it involves behavior, discipline, and emotions. Many struggle because they lack the knowledge or the discipline to create and stick to a plan. Also, the unexpected events of life can disrupt even the best strategies."

Charles: "Understanding Money management is one thing while applying it consistently is another, especially when values aren't always what they seem. Take house prices, for instance—they don't always reflect real value."

GP: "I agree! Still, Money is a valuable tool and just like the tools in our garage we need to learn to handle it efficiently."

Charles: "Undoubtedly! As you taught me, I coach my clients, emphasizing that well-managed Money not only grants security, but also paves the way to a life they envision. Historically, Money has always been a means to trade goods and services. It facilitates transactions and drives economic growth. Money can be traded for anything desired, wanted, or needed. Even in the form of a loan."

GP: "It's deeper than that, Charles! Money helps us realize our dreams through our financial choices. It's the driving force beyond mere transactions that helps us achieve our aspirations."

## THE EVOLUTION OF MONEY

GP: "It's fascinating how Money has evolved, much like cars in our garage. From bartering to digital currency, it's quite a journey! It's like going from horse riding to self-driving cars."

Charles: "Indeed, Money evolves quickly, and we must adapt."

GP: "In the past, people directly swapped goods and services, like trading a chicken for shoes. In my early years, paper Money was in fashion, changing like car models!"

Charles: "Then came plastic Money (credit cards) for spending when your pockets are empty. It sadly keeps many in overdraft mode."

GP: "And now, with online banking and e-transfers, you just point your phone, and the payment's done. It's all about convenience, like having a personal chauffeur for your Money."

Charles: "Indeed! And it seems like we may be moving to crypto Money. This wild child of finance operates on decentralized networks, like Bitcoin and Ethereum."

GP: "Like a skilled mechanic, let's drive safely and responsibly, whether handling cash or cruising the digital highway. The key is to stay grounded and true to our values, making smart financial decisions for a smoother ride."

Charles: "The crypto highway, with its unpredictable twists, reminds us to be vigilant and adaptable for whatever lies ahead." It's like when we talk about time, benefit, and Money. I can't help but think about how life's journey intertwines."

## TIME, BENEFIT, AND MONEY

GP: "Think of your financial education as fine-tuning a car for a race. Just like you invest time and energy to prime it, you trade your skills and knowledge for a paycheck when you enter the job market. The market becomes your racetrack, and your earnings are the rewards.

Charles: "And while we're the drivers, we shouldn't forget that Money's true value lies in its functionality, managed by institutions like the Federal Reserve or the Bank of Canada that ensuring that our economy's engine runs smoothly."

As the two continued their deep dive into the intricacies of finance, the conversation shifted to a pivotal topic that governs our relationship with wealth.

GP: "Managing finance is like maintaining your car. Track its fuel, budget its rides, save for its upgrades, and steer toward your ambitions."

Charles: "You'd be proud—under your guidance, I've kept my financial gears well-oiled, and given my savings the care they deserve. I've come to value and diligently nurture Money, ensuring it'll be there when I need it the most."

GP: "Smart move, son! Taking control of your finances means you're in the driver's seat.

Let me show you how I've tracked my earnings and expenses in my weekly journal. This method has worked wonders for me. I highly recommend that you give it a try!"

We live in a society of unnecessary consumerism, driven by mass-media hype that encourages immediate gratification. We fail to see the price we pay for such behavior."

WHAT IS MONEY? | 11

> **LET'S PLAY: TABULATE YOUR WEEKLY JOURNAL!**
>
> This week, what happened with my Money?
>
> I have earned_____.
>
> My spending was_____.
>
> Net remaining:_____.
>
> I have spent on _____.
>
> It made me happy: YES or NO

Charles: "You're right. The mechanics of finance is no mystery at all. I am committing to maintaining my weekly journal."

## NAVIGATING LIFE WITH MONEY AS YOUR CO-PILOT

GP: "Money is like a faithful companion that grows with care. We've always had a unique way of honoring its role in our lives. The secret of **our family is that Money is more than just a currency; it's a trusted partner, a co-pilot on our life's journey.**"

Charles: "I honor our tradition, GP. Every evening, I come home and 'feed' MONEY my pocket change. It's not just about saving; it's a ritual of respect, a daily reminder of our family's wisdom."

GP: "Ah, that little green pouch your grandmother crafted, each stitch a lesson in value and saving. It warms my heart to see you've grasped Money's power. Our modest ritual is like the modern methods of automated savings—consistent, disciplined, and forward-thinking."

Charles: "I've even incorporated apps replicating our tradition, setting aside small amounts that add up over time."

GP: "Good work son, continue this discipline. Let's show others how to craft themselves a Money pouch and put in their pocket change every day. Imagine the gift it will be."

For Money pouch patterns, see whotookmymoney.ca

---

**NUTS AND BOLTS**

**Money is a valuable tool.**

- It does not have feelings or thoughts. Neither does it judge if you are worthy or not.
- It's meant for spending, saving, investing, and giving our lives a purpose. Use it wisely.
- Money is also the legacy of love, by giving a little.

**What you do with your Money? The choice is yours.**

- Money should be your trusted companion and co-pilot.
- Master the mechanics of finance to unlock infinite opportunities.
- Nurture, respect, and care for your Money.
- Learn and grow with Money's evolving dynamics. Its role has evolved, introducing new opportunities and challenges. It's essential to adapt to these changes.
- Adopt effective financial management. Empowerment comes from it. Failing to do so hands the power over to others.

**Money has no power; the true power lies in how you handle it.**

Truly grasp MONEY as your co-pilot, align it with GP's rules of finance, and you hold the power to revolutionize your financial life.

## GP'S MONEY PRINCIPLES

- Truth creates Money; lies destroy it.
- Look at what you have, not at what you had.
- Prioritize based on your values and needs, not decisions for financial gain.
- Prepare yourself for the unknown—before it takes you by surprise.
- Monitor your spending and manage your Money wisely.

## A LITTLE INSPIRATION

### The Boy and Lady Luck

In a tranquil village of Prosper, young Brin often played by an old stone well with his closest companion MONEY, the little green pouch. One sunny day, while whispering secrets to MONEY near the well's edge, a mischievous gust snatched MONEY from Brin's grasp, sending it spiraling into the depths below.

Panicking, Brin peered into the well, trying to catch a glimpse of his lost friend. As he did, a shimmering figure, Lady Luck, gracefully emerged from the water, cradling MONEY.

"I believe this belongs to you," she said, presenting the little green pouch to a relieved Brin. "But remember, if you wish to keep MONEY by your side, you must nurture it. It's not enough to merely possess Money; one must also understand its value and treat it respectfully."

Brin nodded, clutching MONEY tightly. "I promise, Lady Luck, I'll always cherish and nurture MONEY. I won't let it slip away again."

Lady Luck dissolved into the well with an approving smile, leaving Brin with his cherished friend, MONEY, and a lifelong lesson about its true value.

CHAPTER 2

# FINANCIAL PITFALLS

"Insanity is repeating the same actions, over and over, again and again, and expecting different results."
—ALBERT EINSTEIN

Picture yourself behind the wheel of a car on the winding roads of financial decisions. Every twist and turn, every decision, is significant. Now, imagine there's a deep well right in the middle of the road. This well symbolizes the pitfalls we face on our financial journeys. Drivers who focus on the past may make new mistakes; they risk driving straight into the well.

Repeating our past actions won't steer us clear of that well. To safely navigate around it, we must keep our eyes on the road ahead and our dreams on the horizon. By harnessing knowledge and focusing on our aspirations, we can turn potential pitfalls into steppingstones on our journey to financial prosperity.

**ASK YOURSELF:**

- How do I currently feel about my financial situation?
- Do I believe that Money is hard to care for?
- What would be my financial pitfall?
- What are my fears relating to Money?

As the soft hum of a vintage radio filled the garage, Charles, and GP, surrounded by memories and the tools of the trade, delved into the challenges of today's financial landscape.

GP: "As humans, we often settle in habits and get comfortable with them whether it is right or wrong. For many people, Money issues have become a nightmare."

Charles: "And the 'must-have' mentality of today's society can shift when we recognize our power as consumers, who have a choice in making mindful financial decisions."

GP: "We need to know what we are doing wrong—before doing it right."

Charles: "Correct GP, let's talk about **facts, statistics**, and **myths**, shall we?"

**THE SHOCKING STATE OF PERSONAL FINANCES**

Charles: "Recent reports show that more than half of North Americans live paycheck to paycheck, impacting all income brackets, including high earners. Paying more annual interest on debt than a family of four spend on groceries over the same year."

GP: "This is a significant increase from past decades. It's like most of the cars in North America are barely making it to the next gas station."

Charles: "It is impossible to enjoy life if you constantly worry about finances. Money arguments are the number one cause of divorce."

GP: "Plus, most folks who bundle their debts, especially from credit cards, end up owing more within a year."

Charles: "It looks like handling debt is a tough lesson still being learned."

GP: "It's alarming. I find that today's generation, instead of enjoying life, is buried under the weight of bills. How would they cover their emergencies?"

Charles: "From my reading I found that 4 in 10 adults would have trouble covering a $400 emergency expense."

GP: "It's mind-boggling. The race to keep up and the desire for more have put many in bad positions. Many folks only see the need for a financial *tune-up* after their car has broken down a few times."

Charles: "**Learning the mechanics of finance** is as important as reading a car manual before hitting the road."

GP: "Mistakes like buying things without planning or budgeting for them can quickly lead to overspending."

Charles: "Watch out for the dream stealers. As you taught us, GP, if we know what we want and take care of our Money, we are safeguarded.'"

GP: "Now, imagine believing cars self-repair! Unfortunately, they don't. Similarly, we can't expect our financial problems to resolve magically on their own."

## MONEY TRAPS AND PITFALLS

GP: "In our society, we often believe we deserve the best even if we can't afford it. Also, trusting others with our finances is like letting someone else drive our car. You better know where you're headed."

Charles: "Beware of the financial traps and who is out to get your Money."

GP: "Recognize them, and you'll make better decisions. Watch out for:

- Buy now, pay later offers.
- Emergency payday loans.
- Rent-to-own deals with hidden costs.
- Borrowing against home equity to clear debts but continuing lousy spending habits.

Charles: "It's intriguing how many get caught in financial snares. Often, it's because they lose track of their goals or don't know how to reach them."

GP: "It's never too late. Even those who've faltered can get back on track with determination."

## HARD LESSONS: UNVEILING THE PITFALLS

In the tales ahead, you'll learn how easily we can drift from our dreams and fall into a debt spiral. These narratives highlight the subtle shifts that lead us away from our aspirations, guiding us to sidestep common financial traps, and navigate a clear path toward our dreams.

## FRAUD: TOO GOOD TO BE TRUE, TRUST YOUR INTUITION

Meet Elaine, a teacher in her late forties who attends an investment seminar presented by Edward, a trusted and respected community member. Edward promises a guaranteed, no-risk return of 15% from his managed fund, enticing Elaine and others with the opportunity to retire early. Seduced by the allure of this seemingly golden opportunity, Elaine invests her hard-earned retirement savings of $180,000.

However, as time passes, concerns arise. Elaine realizes she hasn't received any annual reports and decides to withdraw her Money. This is when Edward's true colors are revealed. He offers her only a fraction of her investment, continuously stalling and making excuses.

Ultimately, it is discovered that Edward's investment fund was a fraudulent scheme, with him stealing over $4 million from individuals.

## The Lesson

GP: "Elaine's unfortunate experience underlines the importance of skepticism. Trusting Edward's glowing reputation and alluring 15% return, she fell for the trap. Remember, it likely is a scam if it looks too good to be true. High returns aren't handed out; they're earned. Beware of these phrases in investment pitches:

- No risk, guaranteed profit.
- Ground floor opportunity.
- Limited time offer.
- Paperwork will follow.

## SHOULD YOU LOAN MONEY TO FAMILY MEMBERS?

Paul met with his favorite grandfather to ask him to co-sign a loan. He wanted to buy a brand-new truck with a price tag of $45,000. He said he needed it for work. His grandfather made Paul a personal loan with a 5% rate of return, far better than anything the bank or car dealership would give him.

Paul promised to repay his grandfather $500 monthly until the loan was fully paid. The first month passed, and no payment was made. The following month, Paul lost his job and could not repay his grandfather. Months passed, and Paul hadn't made a single payment. His grandfather decided that Paul had to sell the truck to repay his debt. The truck sold for $38,000, leaving the grandfather short by $7,000 and angry at his grandson.

What do you think happened to this previously close relationship? How do you think the grandfather felt? How do you think the grandson felt?

### The Lesson

GP: "When it comes to family and friends, **do not loan but give**. Then, you receive the joy of giving. When you make a loan, you aren't equal in the relationship, and it is easy for resentments to spring up, especially if the loan can no longer be repaid."

Charles: "I couldn't agree more, GP! I believe it is not our responsibility to pay for other people's dreams."

## SCAMMED OUT OF A DOWN PAYMENT:
### Lessons in Trust and Patience

In this relatable story, we meet Isabelle, a single mother of three, who was thrilled to find a reputable home builder offering a loan with great terms. Excited about the prospect of a new home, she made a $3,000 deposit. However, things took an unexpected turn. Just weeks before closing, the builder's agent called and requested an additional $1,000 for Isabelle to qualify for the loan. Distracted by her mother's emergency surgery, Isabelle met the agent late in the evening, paid the $1,000, and signed the new agreement, unaware of the consequences. Little did she know that by signing the agreement, she unknowingly forfeited her original deposit of $3,000 should she not be able to proceed with the purchase.

A week later, Isabelle was devastated when the builder's agent informed her that she no longer qualified for the loan, leaving her without a place to live and unable to recover her deposit. Struggling just before Christmas, Isabelle reflected on the experience, feeling foolish and betrayed.

### The Lesson

GP: "This story reminds us to remain vigilant. Like driving, always carefully read the road signs, or in this case, the contract. Seek expert advice before signing anything."

## GET IT IN WRITING!

Pearl married young, and for twenty-four years, life was beautiful. She and her husband had three great kids and, by managing their Money, had a lovely home in a great neighborhood with only a few thousand dollars left to pay on the mortgage. Life consisted of laughter, love, and no Money worries. Then it all fell apart.

Pearl moved out of her home with just a few pieces of furniture and her personal belongings. She and her husband verbally agreed that everything they had jointly worked for would be settled once the children left so their lives would not be too disrupted. The equity of their home would be separated equally.

Six years later, Pearl received a legal notice that her husband owed her nothing and was now the family home's sole owner. In tears, Pearl sought legal advice only to discover that one cannot claim marital rights after six years of separation. It was too late; the verbal agreement she had trusted him to keep was not respected. Everything she had worked hard for was gone, and there was no way to get it back.

### The Lesson

GP: "Pearl learned the hard way. Know your rights and act to protect them without delay. In retrospect, she should have consulted a lawyer specializing in marital disputes. Unfortunately, at the time, Pearl worried that doing so might make things worse with her then-husband and that he would be more hostile towards the children. Pearl learned a harsh lesson: get it in writing! Remember: good papers make good friends. Not everyone has the same values, and people change."

Charles: "I agree. It's essential to seek help from a reputable professional in the field. It's an investment that initially involves a cost but will likely keep Money by your side in the long run."

> **NUTS AND BOLTS**
>
> Many feel rushed and pressured to catch up on their dreams, leading to increasing financial challenges. The misconception that time will naturally resolve Money problems can worsen the situation. It's crucial not to find oneself wondering, "Who took my Money?"
> **Avoid traps!**
>
> ☐ Evaluate your financial position TODAY.
>
> ☐ Refrain from blaming external factors; take responsibility.
>
> ☐ Knowledge is **power**. Continually **read** and **learn**.
>
> You are the ideal target for a financial pitfall if you neglect your Money.

**Why don't cars ever have Money problems?**
**– Because they always 'brake' for debts!**

GP: "Before we journey, let's do that exercise. How would you rate yourself on a scale of 1 to 10?

### THE SELF-CHECK!

- I save at least 5%–10% of my yearly earnings.
- I use a budget to manage my spending.
- I have enough Money to cover my monthly expenses.
- I have savings to help with emergencies, worth two to three months of my earnings.
- I check my credit score regularly and use credit wisely.
- Before getting a personal loan, I plan my budget and make sure I can repay it.

FINANCIAL PITFALLS | 23

- I start every year by reviewing my finances and goals.
- Unless something unusual happens, I pay my entire monthly credit card bill.
- If I buy something now to be paid later, I pay it off by the due date.
- Every year, I make a report of my finances to see how I'm doing.

---

**FROM GP'S TOOLBOX: CREATE YOUR MONEY ROSE**

*Take a $5 bill and fold it in half lengthwise. Roll the edges to the center crease. Create the petal shape. Cover a small piece of floral tape around the bottom of the petal to hold the shape. Repeat for all bills.* **Have fun!**

*For complete steps, visit: whotookmymoney.net.*

---

*If crafting a Money rose doesn't resonate with you, find a visualization technique that aligns with your style and inspires your financial journey.*

## A LITTLE INSPIRATON

### The Heart of the Rose

In the heart of Wall Street, a businessman named Joly was always worried about Money. Despite all his wealth and the city's bright lights, he felt heavy with financial stress and couldn't find true peace. This all started to change when he saw a book called *The Monk Who Sold His Ferrari* by Robin Sharma on a park bench.

The book grabbed his attention, and he was drawn to a technique called the "Heart of the Rose."

As daylight filled the city the following day, he sat by his window holding a soft rose, letting its beauty calm him for a few minutes. This became his daily escape, a peaceful spot in his busy life.

This quiet time with the rose helped Joly change his negative thoughts about Money—like "Money is evil"—to positive ones, like "Money is a valuable tool that I will take care of and respect." The more he did this, the better he understood his life. He realized that chasing Money wasn't bothering him; it was his limited thoughts. He was now driven by peace, not fear.

The lessons from Sharma's book hit home for Joly. Just like being careful with the thorns of a rose, reaching success is tough and full of challenges. He could grow stronger with faith, hard work, and a different way of thinking.

CHAPTER 3

# MIND OVER MONEY

"You are today where your thoughts have brought you;
you will be tomorrow where your thoughts take you."
—JAMES ALLEN

*Bad habits are not easily abandoned; the best way to change them is to replace them.*

What you tell yourself reflects your beliefs, which in turn influence your behaviors towards Money. The quality of your thoughts determines the quality of your life. Change old habits and beliefs, feed your mind only positive thoughts, and learn to eliminate those negative beliefs from the past. Prepare for a life without financial worries! That alone is a life journey. Along the way, you will find fulfillment and happiness beyond financial success.

**ASK YOURSELF:**

- Do I have any unhealthy financial habits that I need to change?
- What are my beliefs towards Money—good or bad?

- What apprehensions do I hold regarding finances?
- What resources or tools have helped me establish good financial habits?

On a fine Tuesday evening, Charles found GP in the garage, enveloped in the scent of motor oil and the hum of a vintage Chevrolet. With GP's seasoned hands and wisdom, they fixed cars and imparted lessons about life's core beliefs. They explored the intricate connection between the mechanics of cars and the foundations of values.

## THE IMPORTANCE OF SELF-TALK

GP: "Charles, you know, changing our financial habits is a journey that begins with proper thinking. It's about being more positive. *The Heart of the Rose* meditation technique is a good way to learn how to be less negative. This same transformation can be applied to our financial habits."

Charles: "I understand now. After reading *The Monk Who Sold His Ferrari*, the concept of mental nourishment hits home."

GP: "Think of your mind as an engine; the quality of your thoughts fuels its performance. The brain doesn't distinguish between right and wrong, good, or bad. As children, we are often taught that Money is dirty, there isn't enough of it, and rich people are greedy. These early teachings can affect our financial approach later in life, often leading to less desirable outcomes."

Charles: "Realizing that my thoughts drive my actions has been a game-changer for my finances. Changing my negative thoughts into positive ones has enhanced my daily life and drawn Money towards me! Or maybe it's just my good charm!"

GP: "Remember this Zen proverb—Be a master of the mind not mastered by the mind."

Charles: "Indeed GP, gaining mastery over one's own thoughts is a lifelong endeavor, but I believe it is a rewarding one."

GP: "It's about finding the balance between control and letting go."

## TUNING UP YOUR BELIEFS ABOUT MONEY

GP: "Picture your beliefs as the old classic cars in our garage. Handed down from parents, teachers, family, and friends, these beliefs may have been reliable in their era. But now, they might be restraining you, keeping you from reaching your full potential.

This journey isn't merely a game; it's a roadmap! It's helping us rethink our beliefs about Money and chart a course towards a wealthier destination."

---

**LET'S PLAY: CHANGING NEGATIVE BELIEFS INTO POSITIVE ONES**

- **I was born to fail.** I was born to live a happy life. I have the power to learn financial management and improve my financial situation.
- **I didn't learn about managing Money from my parents or in school:** Even though I wasn't taught Money management, I can learn and access resources now. Professionals and educational tools are available to help me gain financial literacy.
- **The system favors the rich:** The system favors those who live within their means and pay their bills on time. One only needs to use good judgment and discipline.
- **Money doesn't grow on trees:** It's not how much Money you make; it's what you do with it that counts.
- **My car, my house, and my toys equal my success:** The happiness of living without worries and experiencing inner peace is the ultimate success.

GP: "Alright, Charles, think of your mind as a six-cylinder engine: thoughts, faith, emotions, fear, attitude, and passion. Each plays a critical role. This is your financial roadmap, so stick with it."

GP then reached into his toolbox, pulling out a well-worn cheat sheet. He passed it to Charles with a twinkle in his eye.

| | |
|---|---|
| **Thoughts**: | You become what you think! |
| **Faith**: | A leap of faith makes it happen! |
| **Emotions**: | They are like messengers. Listen to them! |
| **Fear**: | It is like a red light! |
| **Attitude**: | The **mindset** we can control daily! |
| **Passion**: | This is your fire within! |

GP: "Now, Charles, the journey doesn't stop at just cruising on the highway, but how you handle those winding roads. The same goes with Money; ask yourself, 'How far can I go?'"

Charles: "It reminds me of how mom has the blue magnet on her fridge that you and Grandma gave her when my parents built our home, it says?"

> **You Never Fail Until You Stop Trying**

GP: "I'm glad the magnet was a good inspiration, as quitting is not an option in our family. We commit to daily improvement."

## COMMITMENT TO CHANGE

Charles: "Habits are not easily abandoned, much like the neglect of regular car maintenance, which can lead to a breakdown."

GP: "Replace bad habits. When the financial pain becomes unbearable, people are driven to find ways and means to transform old thinking processes and to forge new habits and behaviors."

Charles: "It requires courage and commitment to ensure these changes are successful."

GP: "Material assets do not solely quantify the value of life, like the cost of a home or possessions amassed over time. It's equally measured by the joy we find in spending our time, managing our Money, and using our talents to enrich our lives and those of others around us."

## TIME TO REPLACE OLD BELIEFS

GP: "It might be time for your financial beliefs to undergo an oil change.

- Commit to discarding old patterns and adopting empowering behaviors.
- Choose wisely and focus on what truly matters."

---

**LETS PLAY: THE PLEDGE FORM**

*I am ready! Achieving financial happiness is simple, not easy.*

*Today, I embark on a journey of self-discipline with Money.*

I, _____, commit to transforming my financial life.

I, _____, commit to investing in myself.

**I am worth it. I deserve it!**

*Initial here as a symbol of your commitment and pledge*

GP: "Embrace the conviction that with dedication, managing Money is simple, achievable, and fun. Make it a habit to cultivate only positive thoughts and always verify the accuracy of your information. In moments of uncertainty, do not hesitate to seek guidance from a trusted professional in the field."

> **NUTS AND BOLTS**
>
> Our early teachings can shape our beliefs and attitudes toward Money, leading to adverse **outcomes. Break free** from those limiting beliefs and create a healthier relationship with Money.
>
> - Transform your **passion** into **action**.
> - Expect **success** rather than **failure**.
> - Focus on **solutions** rather than **problems**.
> - **Speak** and **act** with **enthusiasm**.
>
> **Enjoy** life with a **positive attitude** and expect a bright future.

**The difference between great people and everyone else is that great people create their lives actively, while everyone else is created by their lives, passively waiting to see where life takes them next. The difference between the two is the difference between living fully and just existing.**

—Michael E. Gerber

### FROM GP'S TOOLBOX: THE DREAM BOARD

Creating a dream board is a great way to visualize your dreams.

- Choose your base (the fridge)
- Gather your inspirations.
- Add interactive elements.

Place your dream board where you'll see it every day. By making it a living, evolving, and interactive display, you keep your dreams vibrant and directly in the flow of your daily life, enhancing the likelihood of realization.

*For a Dream Board Idea visit:* *whotookmymoney.ca*

# A LITTLE INSPIRATION

## When Dreams Become Reality

In the neon-lit streets of the city, this young lady, Destiny, was not so good of a driver; she was nervous at the wheel. During an unexpected side trip, Destiny's direction changed.

She ended up at a big car race with loud crowds. Engines roared, tires skidded, and excitement filled the air. Each turn of the steering wheel, every intelligent risk, and the strong connection between the drivers meant more than a race—it was like a dance full of passion and precision.

In that short moment, Destiny had a wake-up call. Driving wasn't only about getting somewhere; it was about the journey, the beat, and the heartbeat of it. More than a job, it was an art, a true calling.

With this new insight, Destiny chose to change her path. She decided not only to become a great driver but the best there was. She signed up for racing school, practiced on tracks, and dived into the life of a pro driver. She worked hard, and the once unsure driver became a strong competitor on the track.

This was how Destiny made a dream sparked by one race, showing the strength of passion and the wonders that come when you go after your dreams with relentless determination.

After all, this is what life is about: turning your dreams into reality.

CHAPTER 4

# DARE TO DREAM

*"The future belongs to those who believe in the beauty of their dreams."*
—ELEANOR ROOSEVELT

In a world where reality often dims the glow of our innermost dreams, dreamers possess the power to carve out the future. Pursuing our dreams isn't mere fancy—it's a courageous voyage requiring unwavering belief in our potential. Dreams demand resilience in the face of adversity, persistence beyond doubt, and a spirit that illuminates even in the darkest challenges. Dreaming expansively allows us to not only strive for excellence, but also to discover our true selves and our true potential.

**ASK YOURSELF:**

- Which dreams and passions deeply resonate with me?
- Have I identified and ordered my dreams?

- If I had only one year to live, which dream would I follow?
- How do my current actions and financial decisions reflect my dreams?

GP arrived as punctual as ever, eager to impart wisdom. Today, Charles and GP focused on transforming dreams into reality, a topic dear to Charles's heart. Let's unravel the art of setting practical goals.

## DREAMS: THE BLUEPRINT OF AMBITION

GP: "We all have dreams, big or small. No matter life's challenges, we're the guardians of our dreams. Dreams lend us wings. Spark them with belief and action; they shall become reality."

Charles: "Many people hold onto their dreams their entire life without realizing them, simply because they don't take action."

GP: "What's missing is goal setting. Take Walt Disney, for example. When drafting Mickey Mouse, he dreamt of something big and magical. That dream blossomed into Disney World because he diligently worked towards it by setting smart goals."

Charles: "The more defined and precise our goals, the sooner they materialize."

GP: "Consider these three W's:

- **What:** Specify what you desire and you're willing to pay for it.
- **Why:** Comprehend the motive behind your dream.
- **When:** Establish a timeframe for yourself, like two years from now."
- GP and Charles began outlining Charles's dream into an actionable plan.

## SETTING *SMART* GOALS

> **LET'S PLAY: CHARLES'S DREAM OF BUYING A HOME**
>
> - Specific: Looking for a cozy bungalow close to all amenities.
> - Measurable: Committing to save $1K monthly for 36 months, amassing a $36K down payment, plus a bit of interest.
> - Attainable: Watching the market for homes that wouldn't take up more than 35% of his paycheck.
> - Realistic: Looking for a property with a potential income opportunity, such as a rentable basement.
> - Time: Aiming to own a home in two years, with a 10% down payment saved up.

GP: "Like your grandmother and I did in the past when we wanted to buy our first home, Charles we've just transformed your dream into a tangible goal! Now, let's consider another goal. Perhaps you could aim to invest an extra 3% of your earnings in five years. As a financial advisor, you'd adhere to our standards and set an example."

Charles: "My growth mantra is simple: 'How high can I grow?' It keeps me focused and disciplined. I have set up a cheat sheet as a memory aid."

GP: "Your innovative approach never fails to impress me! And to keep you on track, let me share a piece of wisdom that has guided me on many financial ventures."

| When you set a goal, be **SMART** about it: | |
|---|---|
| **S**pecific: | not vague |
| **M**easurable: | help you stay on track |
| **A**ttainable: | possible |
| **R**ealistic: | within reason |
| **T**imely: | set in a reasonable time frame |

## PURSUING YOUR DREAMS

Charles: "I believe those who achieve their dreams possess a robust belief in themselves and are always primed for action."

GP: "I agree, they don't shy away from challenges; instead, they embrace them. They've conditioned their mind to make any obstacle appear smaller and more manageable."

> **NUTS AND BOLTS**
>
> - It all starts with a dream. It's important to dream.
> - Transform your dreams into action with SMART goals.
> - Apply the 3 W's: What, Why, and When for effective planning.
> - Maintain self-discipline; your biggest reward will be seeing your dreams come true.
>
> Let Walt Disney's legacy reminds you: whatever your dream, take action—anything is achievable.
>
> Create your dream board as it's the dashboard of your future, guiding you towards your greatest aspirations. Embrace the belief that all is within reach, and drive towards your dreams with the pedal firmly to the metal.

> "The stock market is filled with individuals who know the price of everything, but the value of nothing."
> **PHILIP FISHER**

To win at the Money Game

## These are the 7 golden rules of finance!

- **F** acilitate your financial education — to control financial destiny
- **I** nitiate a new way of thinking — debunk the myth
- **N** ever live above your means — BUDJET— Buffet multi-billionaire
- **A** pply the basic financial principles — Dream 20/ Plan 30/ Action 50
- **N** ever forget to pay yourself first — You #1
- **C** ome to experience the magic of compound interest — Retirement freedom
- **E** liminate debt — impact on your physical health

## A LITTLE INSPIRATION
### Breaking Free from the Loop: A Butterfly's Tale

In the town of Crawlsville, Curly the caterpillar lived a life of repetitive loops, tracing the same paths and patterns on the rim of a familiar flowerpot. It was all he knew, and much like many of us, his days felt bound by routine, like a record stuck on the same old track. His friends, the other caterpillars, also seemed content in their endless dance, but with his insatiable curiosity, Curly started dreaming of more. Whispers of change echoed through the leaves, with stories about caterpillars turning into colorful butterflies flying in the air.

One day, inspired by a sunset, Curly made a daring decision. No longer would he remain confined to his predictable loops. It was cocoon time! He wrapped himself in a silken embrace, seeking the magic transformation legends spoke of.

The days within were a time of reflection and metamorphosis. Curly envisioned a life where he soared above treetops, danced with petals in the wind, and explored lands beyond Crawlsville. It was challenging; the cocoon was dark and snug, but with every challenge, Curly grew stronger.

And then, the moment arrived. With newfound strength and an unyielding spirit, Curly, no longer just a caterpillar, burst forth as Sir Flutters, a majestic butterfly. His wings, a canvas of colors, carried stories of his dreams.

Returning to Crawlsville, Sir Flutters became a beacon of hope, inspiring others with his tale. He'd share: "Life may often feel like a loop, but within each of us lies the power to change our tune. Dare to dream, and let your spirit take flight!"

So, whenever you feel cornered by life's routines, remember Curly's tale. There's a transformative adventure awaiting, and it begins with the courage to embrace change. Break free, spread those wings, and find your rhythm in the vast sky of possibilities.

**CHAPTER 5**

# THE FINANCIAL TOOL KIT, PART 1

### GET BACK TO BASICS

*"Your net worth to the world is usually determined by what remains after your bad habits are subtracted from your good ones."*
—BENJAMIN FRANKLIN

It is imperative to safeguard your essential documents in a secure place and on the cloud. We will show you how to create a simple tag system and capture a snapshot of your financial worth at a precise date, known as your *net worth*. This snapshot is a powerful tool for planning your financial strategy and pinpointing where to focus your efforts. By understanding and managing your net worth, you are ready to reinvent your finances and unlock a world of possibilities.

**ASK YOURSELF:**

- How am I truly doing financially?
- Am I in control of my Money?

- Do I have a financial plan in place?
- What is the significance of a net worth statement?
- Do I fully comprehend my financial documents?

On a bright Sunday afternoon, Charles and GP were busy changing tires on the old Cadillac. The air was filled with the distinct smell of rubber and nostalgia. As Charles fondly thought of moments with Jessie, his life partner, he noticed GP's briefcase on the workbench. Among the tools and tires, a financial discussion was about to unfold.

## ORGANIZING YOUR DOCUMENTS

Charles: "I admit, I've let a 'financial junk drawer' pile up. I often toss my bills and such in it without much thought."

GP: "Make time to transform your clutter into an organized filing system. Here is how I see it."

### Financial Planning
Budget—map
Net worth statements
Cashflow
Financial goals
Bank statements
Monthly credit card statement(s)
Pay stubs (income sources)

### Insurance
Accident / Health insurance
Mortgage / Tenant insurance
Car insurance
Income replacement and disability coverage
Life insurance
Critical illness coverage

## Legal Documents
    Contracts: marriage, divorce, etc.
    Bank loans and other loans
    Holdings: deeds to property
    Will and testament
    Income tax documents (keep six years of tax documents)

## Savings and Investments
    Bank accounts
    Term deposits, certificates
    Non-registered investment plans
    RRSPs, TFSA, FHSA, RESP, RDSP and pension documents

## Housing and Transport
    Home (lease, mortgage
    Car bills
    Electricity, heating, phone
    Important bills (furniture etc.)
    Medical bills
    Property taxes, Debts
    Personal loan
    Credit cards
    Line of credit (LOC)
    Family loan

## THE SNAPSHOT: YOUR NET WORTH STATEMENT

GP: "Now that we've tuned up your financial filing system, let's dive into the topic of net worth, the real measure of our financial strength. Understanding your net worth is like doing a thorough check-up on your car. You must know what's working well and what may need attention. It's better to do the dirty work now than to break down on the highway."

Charles: "Absolutely! A net worth statement captures our financial situation at a precise date. It reveals important clues about where we should concentrate our financial planning efforts for the future."

GP pulled out a sheet of paper from his toolbox and placed it in front of Charles.

GP: "Net worth statements are also helpful for other purposes, such as applying for a mortgage, a credit card, a car loan, or even your children's college financial aid.

Think back to when I showed you how to split the paper into two parts: assets, which are what you own, and liabilities, what you owe."

**Assets: list everything of value that you own**

- Cash and cash equivalents: certificates of deposit, Money market accounts, bank accounts, and your piggy bank.
- Investments: stocks, bonds, mutual funds, savings bonds, segregated funds, TFSA, FHSA, and others
- Retirement funds: retirement plans, RRSPs, RRIFs, and company pension plans. Include only the amounts you are fully vested in.
- Real estate: your home and any other real estate or personal property such as a boat, cars, RVs, etc.
- Household and personal goods: furnishings, jewelry, art, collectibles, and antiques. Use the estimated fair market value (the price a rational buyer would pay). For cars, use the black book value.

**Liabilities: list all amounts you owe**

- Loans: mortgage, student loans, bank loans, and car loans
- Credit card balances: bank, store, and gas cards
- Taxes owed: real estate taxes or income taxes

▸ Any miscellaneous amounts that you owe

Charles: "This guide is amazing! Knowing the strengths and the weaknesses of one's financial health is just like keeping a car in good condition."

GP: "Keep in mind, net worth isn't just about counting the cash you have; it's about getting a full picture of your financial situation. How well are you doing financially?

Let's try this! Grab a piece of paper and walk around your home and list every valuable you own. It might take some time, but it will be well worth the effort."

After a few days, Charles returned with a piece of paper that he handed to GP.

Charles: "Check this out! I did the math, subtracted my debts from what I own, and voilà! My assets outweigh my liabilities, like having more gas in the tank than miles to travel. My net worth is in the green, and it feels great!"

*(This statement is a snapshot of one's financial status at a specific time.)*

GP: "It's essential to regularly update our net worth statement as asset values, debts, and personal situations change. If ever the number shows a negative *(more liabilities than assets)*, don't despair. With my effective budgeting from the *Financial Tool Kit*, you'll get back on track quickly."

Charles: "You're right! At first, when I was reviewing my net worth, let me tell you, it was like trying to change the oil without a wrench. The assets were easy, like counting all the shiny new parts. But then there were the liabilities. Those are like the repair bills waiting to bring you down! I realized that I had missed including some items."

GP: "I've been in that spot myself. Understanding where you stand financially today sets the stage for a solid retirement. Start saving young, then by age forty, you should aim for a net worth double your annual net salary."

Charles: "And net worth is the Money you'd have left after you sold everything you owned and paid off all debts."

GP: "Exactly. Picture your financial journey like a car race. Your net worth is the finish line."

Charles: "I've fastened my seatbelt for this ride! Learning to navigate the financial highway isn't just about Money for me. It's about securing a future with my partner, Jessie. We have big dreams, and I want to ensure we're on track. If you have a wise tip on improving my net worth, I'm all ears!"

GP: "OK. Think of a car stuck in the mud. If your net worth is spinning its wheels, it's time to apply some financial traction. Put in a bit more effort and cut back on expenses. It'll boost your savings and reduce your debts—now that's a journey tuned for success."

Charles: "Starting with a financial review and then celebrating with a candlelight dinner is a wonderful way to stay focused on our financial targets."

> Why did the dollar bill take the penny out for a candlelight dinner?
> Because it makes "cents" to occasionally enjoy a "change" of scenery!

GP: "You've got the right idea. Adding a dash of humor and fun to our financial discussions will keep the process enjoyable."

Charles: "Do you remember those Sunday afternoons we spent laughing and learning over that old board game?"

With a twinkle in the eye, GP reached into his toolbox and pulled out a well-worn board. Charles's face lit up, seeing that cherished board game preserved through all these years. And the two buddies finished the night playing and sharing laughter.

> **LET'S PLAY: CASH-ONLY SPENDING CHALLENGE**
>
> Try the proposed challenge as we move on to the second part of the Financial Tool Kit. The purpose is to embark on a one-week journey to mindful spending. By using only cash for your transactions, you'll engage more deeply with each purchase and become acutely aware of your spending habits.
>
> - Each morning, assess your planned expenses and carry only enough cash to cover them.
> - Leave all credit/debit cards and cheque books in a secure place at home. If you need one for your sanity, wrap a paper around it and write in bold: IS THIS AN EMERGENCY?
> - Next, note the difference in your spending behavior and observe any changes in your financial awareness."

Charles: "Why do this, GP?

GP: "After the challenge, take some time to reflect on the experience. Did you spend less? How did it feel to part with physical Money? This week, consider writing your observations in your journal to track your spending habits. Seeing the cash leaving your hands can often lead to surprising savings."

In a world where financial stability often eludes many, Charles had just wrapped up a meeting with client Jamie that understand the importance of budgeting—even for those already doing well with their investments and carrying no debt. Here's a glimpse into their conversation that reveals how a budget can bring about even greater financial clarity and control.

GP: "By the way, son, how did the meeting with Jamie go?"

Charles: "Better than expected. She was worried about her housing, but after reviewing her finances, she was in a better shape than she realized. It's understandable. Her husband had always been the one looking after their finances. Unfortunately, due to his illness, he's now living in a long-term care home. Jamie had never done a budget before; she was worried that she wouldn't have enough Money to pay for everything. I explained that having a budget meant peace of mind because she would know where every dollar goes."

GP: "She must have been relieved!"

Charles: "Yes, very! We've then established a balanced budget. We've dialed down her 'pay yourself first' approach from 30% to 10% and redistributed the difference: 5% more to housing, easing her rent worries, and split the remainder between an emergency fund and her long-term aspirations. Plus, I introduced her to the concept of a dream board to visualize her financial ambitions."

GP: "Sounds like Jamie is more relaxed now! It's important for everyone to recognize the benefits of a well-prepared budget, no matter their financial situation.

## NUTS AND BOLTS

Be organized! It will save hours and give you more time for fun and less time spent worrying about Money.

Take the time to assess your financial health by calculating your net worth:

- List all your assets: everything you own that has value.
- List all your liabilities: all your debts and obligations you owe.
- Find your net worth: subtract your total liabilities from your assets: net worth = assets − liabilities.

If your financial picture differs from where you want it to be, BE PATIENT!

Start today, one change at a time.

Remember to invest in yourself; you are worth it.

## A LITTLE INSPIRATION

### The Legend of Lenny and the Lustrous Butterflies

In a quaint town, Bin and his best friend, a little green pouch named MONEY, held close all the cash saved for dreams yet to be realized. One day, they ventured to a nearby village, drawn by tales of magical butterflies whose wings could weave the most detailed of budgets with their enchanting touch.

When they arrived, these magical butterflies greeted Bin and MONEY, each fluttering their wings and spinning threads of financial wisdom through the air. The butterflies, with their mystical aura, whispered secrets of Money management to Bin, guiding his hands as he crafted a budget that balanced his needs and wants like never before.

The magic of the butterflies didn't just lay in their beauty or their dance in the sky, but in their ability to turn the boring task of budgeting into an art form. Under their guidance, Bin learned to allocate, save, and foresee, transforming his once careless approach to his finances into a strategic dance of numbers and goals.

As days passed, the once ordinary green pouch began to glow, brimming not just with cash but with potential and promise. Bin discovered that with the help of these magical beings, budgeting wasn't just about saving his cash; it was about setting the stage for a future filled with wonders.

In the end, the reward was twofold: a well-fed pouch MONEY and a heart full of hope. Bin's story spread across lands, a testament to the enchanting power of planning and the boundless reward that awaits those who embrace the magic of wise financial stewardship.

Everything is possible; just add a little magic.

CHAPTER 6

# THE FINANCIAL TOOL KIT, PART 2

*"Don't tell me where your priorities are.
Show me where you spend your Money
and I'll tell you what they are."*
—JAMES GP. FRICK

Planning for your financial future can be as exciting as planning a great road trip. Think about it: mapping out the route, setting sights on the horizon, and taking action to turn dreams into reality. We invest months into vacation planning, so why not do the same for our life goals? Once your dreams are set as SMART goals, create a budget that suits you, and be ready to adjust along the way. This process can be simple and fun. With the right mindset and dedication, you'll see how achievable your financial aspirations can be.

**This Tool Kit is five easy steps—GP's Healthy Money Cycle:**

1. SNAPSHOT – 2. MAP IT – 3. COMPARE – 4. ADJUST – 5-REVIEW

**ASK YOURSELF:**
- ▶ What have I always wanted to do but haven't yet accomplished?
- ▶ Do I have a detailed and realistic budget? Am I sticking to it?
- ▶ Which non-essential expenses can I reduce or eliminate?

As Charles and GP gathered in the garage, GP was prepared to share his Financial Tool Kit approach, a navigational aid for the financial journey. They're about to impart essential strategies for staying on track and advancing toward one's financial goals.

GP: "Charles, consider my Money Tool Kit as crucial as your car's toolkit. This toolkit encompasses a vital five-step process."

**GP'S HEALTHY MONEY CYCLE**
- ▶ **SNAPSHOT: Net worth.** This is your financial starting point.
- ▶ **MAP IT: Budgeting** helps you chart a solid financial direction.
- ▶ **COMPARE: Assess your** spending and saving habits.
- ▶ **ADJUST: Refine and fine-tune** your financial plan as needed.
- ▶ **REVIEW: Accept** honestly the consequences of your financial decisions and their impact.

Charles: "GP, it's astounding that three-quarters of the working population don't plan or track their expenses. It's like trying a cross-country drive without a map!"

GP: "Indeed, Charles. Many overlooks budgeting, not realizing it's the key to financial independence. Just as you need a map for the road, you need a budget to guide your income and expenses toward the best choices."

Charles: "Absolutely, and managing our spending is crucial, no matter our financial situation."

GP: "I get where you're coming from, son. But steer clear of those *starvation budgets*—they're like crash diets that never stick. You'll end up where you started, chasing old habits. Tailor your budget to fit your lifestyle and make it sustainable. Remember, budgeting is a skill refined over time. The more attention you give it, the smoother your financial journey becomes. Remember: overspending means overworking. Escape that vicious cycle; balance is the key."

Charles: "A budget is like a roadmap, complete with rest areas, exciting detours, and yes, even the occasional treat. Can we ensure there are pit stops for life's little pleasures, like chocolates?"

GP: "Chocolate pit stop it is, Charles!"

Charles: "By meticulously allocating each dollar of my income, I ensure every dollar is purposefully spent."

GP: "Correct! Now, start allocating your income into the expense category. The first payee is YOU! Saving should be your priority because it acts as your financial fuel."

Charles: "Now, let's take that budget for a spin and see where it can take us!"

As they settled in with just a pen, paper, and calculator app —the two buddies transformed budgeting from a chore to an adventure. With each number crunched and category defined, they charted a course for both immediate and distant financial goals. The session was filled with laughter and easy-to-understand analogies, transforming the daunting task of budgeting into something like planning an exciting road trip.

Charles: "This budget is truly revealing. It's like switching on the high beams to spot the roadblocks ahead! I can already see some expenses I might need to reconsider. But it raises a question: what am I willing to give up for it?"

GP: "That's an excellent question! You might cut back on frequent social nights out by inviting your friends over for a movie night and popcorn instead. These are the choices you make today for a smoother ride tomorrow."

Consider these strategies:

- Seek ways to increase your income. Could you ask for a raise? Or take a rewarding side job?
- Regularly revisit your expenses. Is there anything you could reduce or remove entirely? Over time, this will help lessen unnecessary desires.
- Make sure your investments are performing well. Are they providing the best possible returns? These steps can significantly improve your financial health."

Throughout their talk, Charles and GP went deeper into the budgeting process. They allocated each portion of Charles's income, balancing immediate needs and future aspirations. Every expenditure was examined critically: does this make me happy? Can I cut back without affecting my quality of life? The session was more enlightening and fun than Charles had expected. It was not just a budget but an actual blueprint for success.

GP: "To accelerate your financial progress, increase your monthly percentage. To facilitate this, adjust other areas of your budget. The total allocation should always equal 100% of your net income."

## MY BUDGET *(sample)*

| Income: | | Expense Category Guideline | |
|---|---|---|---|
| Spouse #1: $3,440 | $3,440 | Savings / Investment | 10% |
| Spouse #2: $4,350 | $4,350 | Housing | 35%–40% |
| **Total Net Income:** | **$7,790** | Food | 5%–15% |
| | | Transport | 8%–10% |
| | | Clothing | 4%–7% |
| | | Education / Medical | 5% |
| | | Insurance | 5% |
| | | Personal / Debts or other Activities | 7%–10% |

| Expenses | | | |
|---|---|---|---|
| Pay yourself first | **$770** | Petty Cash | $200 |
| Mortgage | $2,220 | Auto insurance | $200 |
| Car loan | $500 | Auto fuel | $300 |
| Property tax | $120 | Auto maintenance | $180 |
| House insurance | $170 | Clothing & Accessories | $200 |
| Utilities: heat, light…. | $320 | Entertainment | $100 |
| Cell phone | $80 | Medical / dental / vision care | $100 |
| Education | $140 | Savings for new car | $150 |
| Home maintenance | $420 | Dining out | $130 |
| Household furnishings | $250 | Internet access | $90 |
| Groceries | $950 | Life insurance | $200 |
| **Total monthly expenses: $7,790** | | | |

Charles: "Thanks, GP! I feel like a seasoned navigator now. And with today's tech, I'll add my twist by going digital with Mint from Intuit. It's an app that resonates with my generation."

GP: "Excellent! Whatever route you take, whatever budgeting system you use, the destination remains the same. Whether it's your app

Mint.com or your mom's trusted Excel spreadsheet, it is important to start plotting your spending plan."

Charles: "Let's focus on the savings category. It's vital for growing our investment portfolio."

GP: "How do you feel about adjusting this to optimize your long-term financial health? Let's examine your discretionary spending, such as dining out and entertainment. Could you be flexible? Do these expenses align with what truly brings you joy, or should you redirect some funds towards your savings goals without compromising your quality of life?"

Charles: "Well, I love my gourmet coffee, but I guess I could brew it at home more often. That could funnel a bit more into my travel fund, which is a passion of mine."

GP: "Smart trade-offs have a significant impact. Now, let's discuss your emergency fund. It's crucial for life's unexpected turns. Do you feel prepared in this regard?"

Charles: "I've been contemplating shifting some *new car savings* to strengthen my emergency fund."

GP: "Let's compare our spending habits with our saving habits and our financial goals, shall we?"

Charles: "I've been diligent with my budget, though I occasionally indulge in buying tech gadgets on impulse."

GP: "Be aware of impulse buying is key. Do these gadgets enhance your quality of life or steer you away from your saving goals? It's smart to wait a bit before making any spur-of-the-moment purchases. It helps distinguish between 'want' and 'need.' How consistent have you been with that?"

Charles: "My savings have been steady. A fixed amount is automatically transferred from my salary, which has been incredibly helpful."

GP: "That's an excellent approach. Setting up automatic transfers helps to have a financial discipline. What about your discretionary spending, like nights out and hobbies?"

Charles: "I've been keeping within limits, though I admit, sometimes I go overboard with dining out."

GP: "It's all about balance, son. Consider setting a 'fun' category for dining and hobbies within your budget. Once it's spent, you wait until the next month. This could help you enjoy your hobbies without guilt or financial strain. And, how about tracking your expenses—how has using Mint helped you identify patterns in your spending?"

Charles: "It's been a game-changer. It highlighted how much I spent on subscription services, some of which I rarely use."

GP: "Subscriptions to your TV channel or magazine can indeed add up. It's wise to review regularly and cancel what you don't use. Now, let's address the essentials. Have you been able to cover all your basic needs comfortably within the budget we've set?"

Charles: "Yes, the essentials are covered. Though, I've noticed I may have overestimated my grocery category. I could probably cut back there and direct those savings to my emergency fund."

GP: "Adjusting as you go—that's the spirit of a proactive budgeter. One last thing, Charles, how does your budget reflect your values and lifestyle goals?"

Charles: "It's allowing me to save for a down payment on the house, pin on my dream board. And I still have room for a little chocolate indulgence, which is non-negotiable. It's small but significant for my sanity!"

GP: "And that's perfectly fine. Budgeting isn't about deprivation; it's about making informed choices that ensure you can enjoy life while securing your financial future. Our budgets are often reflections of our priorities and dreams. Keep up the good work, son, and keep making every dollar count."

In their warm conversation, the two buddies shared a lively discussion about smart spending, the value of saving, and the possibility of enjoying life's joys while reaching for their financial dreams. They agreed that with technology's help, managing Money is an ongoing and enjoyable journey.

## FINANCIAL ACCOUNT GUIDE

GP: "To ensure you stay on track quickly, divide your Money into distinct accounts and sub-accounts.

Here's how to categorize:

**Savings for wants.** Funds are allocated for future, non-essential purchases, for example, a TV, a coffee table, or designer shoes. Visualize these items on a dream board and plan to purchase them at a set time.

**Incidental expenses.** Occasional expenses that don't occur regularly, for example, gifts and travel expenses. If your budget is well-managed, merge this with your savings.

**Checking Account.** Survival needs include, for example, shelter, groceries, clothing, medical, and transportation. *Monitor* and adjust this account regularly to ensure your needs align with your income.

**Variable expenses** that vary monthly—*monitor.*

**Fixed expenses** are consistent each month, for example, rent, insurance, and car payments. *Set as a sub-account from your chequing account.*

**Investments.** Asset accounts that will grow over time to eventually become your income, such as, stocks, bonds, and retirement accounts. *Prioritize* contributions to this account to secure your financial future.

**Emergency funds.** Savings for unavoidable unexpected events, such as, car repairs and medical bills. Keep this fund easily accessible but separate from other accounts to resist the temptation of tapping into it for non-emergencies.

**Cash flow (your pocket Money).** Small, readily available funds for daily minor expenses, such as, milk and casual snacks. Keep handy; set aside an amount each week to prevent overspending.

Automating your finances by categorizing them into these accounts can simplify your budgeting process, make savings more systematic, and help you manage your Money more effectively."

Charles: "I used to have a separate savings account without a bank card to control impulse spending, but this structured approach is much clearer and seems more efficient."

GP: "Just imagine creating your financial feast. Your income is the main ingredient, your necessities are the everyday spices, and your wants are the exotic flavors you add sparingly. Over time, you'll perfect your recipe."

Charles: "Some people come to me, worried they've overspent. But usually, they want too much too soon. Your Financial Tool Kit is the recipe book guiding a person to a well-balanced, satisfying financial banquet."

GP: "I'm totally with you Charles, budgeting is like a culinary art mixing, measuring, and waiting for flavors to develop. You can't expect to have a rich chocolate cake immediately, but with time and patience, it will be the sweetest thing you've ever tasted."

## ADJUST (REVIEW)

GP: "Let me share a simple method to streamline our finances: Audit 1, 2, and 3. It's like turning bill management into a lucrative role.

1. **Save your receipt.** Remember the old baseball cap I gave you? Use it as a collection point for all your receipts, no matter how small the purchase.

2. **Sort and tabulate.** At week's end, organize these receipts into your budget categories.

3. **Adjust your expenses.** Feeling overwhelmed? Too much work? Aim to collect fewer receipts.

Even minor expenses add up—like gum, coffee, and chocolate. It's wise to track every purchase for a clear financial picture."

Charles: "By going digital with my budgeting, it automatically categorizes expenses and warns me if I'm about to overspend. I enjoy the pace."

## AUDIT 1-2-3

GP: "Vigilance in tracking all expenses, manually or digitally, is critical. Regularly reviewing our spending helps adjust our budget to align with our financial goals. Reflect monthly on:

- Did this expense make me happy?
- Do I need to allocate that much for car accessories?
- Oh boy, I went over budget on takeout this month.

"By staying honest to ourselves and meticulously monitoring our expenses, we can quickly become a financial superhero of our finances. Believing in success is half the battle won."

Charles: "Following this approach, I've noticed I was overspending on car fresheners. I've since redirected that Money."

GP: "Enjoying life while managing Money wisely keeps us on track. Consider these strategies as your fiscal navigation system, ensuring each step is taken with purpose and direction.

## NUTS AND BOLTS

- Dreams are the groundwork.
- SMART goals make dreams a reality.
- Achieving dreams requires a roadmap.
- Success is found in discipline, regular practice, and persistence.
- Honesty in budgeting is the key.
- Adhere to the cycle: spend less, save more.
- The process includes constant review, comparison, commitment, and adjustments. Call it Audit 1–2–3.
- With proper planning and execution, you can truly laugh all the way to the bank.

Review and compare; commit and adjust.

Seeking guidance from a financial coach can further accelerate your journey.

GP: Within us rages a battle between light and darkness. The victor is determined not by fate but by the choices we make daily.

- Have you ever gone out to dinner or bought a gift beyond your means because you didn't want a friend to know that Money was tight?
- How about justifying your spending binge when you are angry with your spouse?
- Have you lied to yourself about having Money to buy something when you know you don't?"

> "Earth provides enough to satisfy every man's needs, but not every man's greed."
> —GANDHI

## A LITTLE INSPIRATION

### A Cherokee Legend: The Eternal Duel Within

Deep within the heart of Cherokee lies a tale that resonates with the rhythm of our very souls. It speaks of two wolves, forever locked in a dance of dominance. A beacon of Good, one wolf radiates love, hope, and serenity. The other, a shadow of Evil, is consumed by anger, jealousy, and bitterness.

Each of us carries these two wolves inside, always wrestling, always contending for our spirit's direction.

A young tribe member, wide-eyed and contemplative, once asked an elder, "Which wolf prevails, Grandfather?"

Gazing into the horizon, the elder responded with a depth that seemed to pull from the ages, "The one you choose to nourish."

This tale, echoing through time, underscores a profound truth: our every thought and deed fuels one of these wolves. The Good wolf thrives when we act with kindness, empathy, and understanding. But when anger, envy, and resentment take hold, the Evil wolf wins.

In the tapestry of our existence, may we recognize the power of choice, for it is through our decisions that we either illuminate our path or cast shadows upon it.

CHAPTER 7

# NEEDS AND WANTS!

*"You can never get enough of what you don't need to make you happy."*
—ERIC HOFFER

When dealing with Money, needs are expenses that are necessary to survive. Wants are expenses which you could do without.

Differentiating between needs and wants is essential because it helps us make smart financial decisions. Once our needs are taken care of and we've saved some Money, we can think about fulfilling our wants. It's all about balance and ensuring the essentials are covered before indulging in luxuries.

**ASK YOURSELF:**

- Do I make informed and conscious spending choices?
- Do I stick to my shopping list without making unplanned purchases?
- Can I give up something if I trim my budget?
- Do I think twice and do my homework before buying?

- Do I consider buying gently used as opposed to brand new?
- When in doubt, do I ask the opinion of an expert?

As the sun dipped below the horizon, casting a warm glow across the garage, GP and Charles concluded their day's work. The air was thick with the scent of motor oil and the sounds of tools fading into silence. Yet, one crucial idea lingered—the distinction between needs and wants.

GP: "One of the key features to taking control of our Money is knowing the difference between needs and wants. That can be tough, as marketers spend a fortune convincing us they are the same."

Charles: "**Needs** are the absolute essentials for our survival. They encompass things like food, shelter, and essential clothing. Let's not forget about medical care, especially when our health is on the line."

GP: "Exactly, these are non-negotiable expenses, and without them, our survival and ability to earn an income could be at risk. We could also include transportation as a need in our modern world.

"Let me tell you how I understand it. They typically include:

- **Healthy food:** We need to eat to survive.
- **Shelter:** A place to live is an essential requirement.
- **Clothing:** Basic clothing to protect from the elements.
- **Health care:** Medications, medical insurance, doctor's visits.
- **Transportation:** A way to get to work or school."

Charles: "**Wants**, on the other hand, are those emotional urges that often get the better of our practical judgment. When our wants take control, our spending gets out of balance. My wants must be aligned with my dreams, placed on my dream board, and included in my budget. A good want should improve my quality of life."

GP: "It's all about enjoying the journey and not rushing for instant gratification. This reminds me of the answer of a wise mother to her daughter: 'Mom, would leather shoes be a want or a need?' The mother replied: 'If they were a need, you would know.'"

Charles: "True needs are self-evident."

GP: "Here's one way I figure out my wants: if I earn $22 per hour and want to buy something that costs $22, is this worth an hour of my time and salary. I ask myself those two questions:

- How many hours do I have to work to pay for it?
- Is it worth the time out of my life?"

## DECODING NEEDS AND WANTS

GP: "Now, try identifying your needs and wants. Write them down using the chart below. This will help you understand better and fine-tune your intuition, a key tool for achieving your goals."

| LET'S PLAY: IS IT A NEED (X) OR A WANT (XX)? | | |
|---|---|---|
| Leather jacket | | XX |
| New work clothes | X | |
| Designer jeans | | XX |
| Snow tires | X | |
| Sports car | | XX |
| Winter coat | X | |
| Scented pillar candle | | XX |

## LEARN TO BE FRUGAL

GP: "Charles, remember our discussion about your first car? The temptation of that flashy sports car versus the sensible choice of the reliable sedan?"

Charles: "Of course. I yearned for the adrenaline rush of the sports car but settled for the sedan's reliability!"

GP: "Exactly, that's the core of frugality: distinguishing your 'high-speed' desires from your 'steady pace' needs."

Their shared understanding of balancing wants and needs fueled the laughter echoing through the garage, a life lessons they shared.

## SMART STRATEGIES FOR SAVVY SPENDING

### Before you spend, Ask Yourself the following:

- Do I need it or want it?
- What other costs are involved?
- How many hours do I have to work to pay for it?
- Am I buying this to compensate for something else?

### Avoid Temptation

- Don't go shopping when you feel emotional.
- Never buy groceries when you are hungry.
- Don't go into that expensive store you know you can't afford (why torture yourself?).
- Sleep on it before you buy. Even when online shopping.
- Out of sight, out of mind—avoiding temptation can prevent impulsive purchases.

### Plan Ahead. Once your basic needs are met,

- Prioritize your wants and write them down.

- Place your wants on your dream board.
- Establish a plan to get your wants.
- Make sure it is included in your budget.

### BIG TICKET COST: THE DREAM BOAT

> "If we could sell our experiences for what they cost us, we'd be millionaires."
> —Abigail Van Buren

Suzie and Ron had a blast on their friend's boat and decided they wanted one of their own. They got caught up in the excitement and impulsively bought a brand-new boat at a boat show. They thought they could manage the costs by tightening their belts and relying on their credit cards. But soon, they realized that owning a boat came with additional expenses. They needed a larger vehicle to tow it. There were marina fees, maintenance and fuel to consider. They bought an SUV and had to work longer hours to cover the extra costs. Unfortunately, they didn't have much time to enjoy their boat and only went boating a few times that summer. Then, a friend told them about a beautiful cottage on a nearby lake. They started to think about the financial burden of the boat and realized they could have a more relaxed lifestyle if they sold it. They boldly decided to sell the boat, stop paying marina and insurance fees, and sell their SUV. With the Money they saved, they were able to buy the cottage instead. Now, they have more time to enjoy each other's company at the lake and spend less time working. Now they also have an appreciating asset they can pass down to their loved ones.

### DREAMING OF OPEN WATERS

Charles: "I found the perfect boat! It's $35,500, with $10,000 from my savings and monthly payments of $450. I've got it mapped out!"

GP: "Hold on, Captain! How about anchoring those desires and steering toward financial freedom? Remember your vintage car spree? All was smooth until repair bills made it costlier than its purchase!"

Charles: "I get your point, but a boat, think of the joy of it! Isn't that what life's about?"

GP: "I'm not telling you to abandon your dreams but to consider all costs; maybe there's a smarter way to get there."

Charles: "You're right; maybe I will rent one a couple of times during the summer."

GP: "Smart thinking!" There could also be another solution.

> **LET'S PLAY: READY TO SET SAIL?**
>
> Crunching numbers could buy a $14,000 used boat and save you $450/month. You could have a newer boat in four years, all paid for! You would be sailing on smooth financial waters. Think of your wallet as your vessel and steer it wisely.
>
> As GP reached into his seasoned toolbox, he handed Charles a paper: "Check this out. It's your guide to smart purchases."

## BUY OUT OF SEASON

- A car: Consider buying used cars and have them checked by a mechanic. If purchasing a new one, plan to keep it for the long term.
- Verify the manufacturer's suggested retail price (MSRP) to avoid overpaying.
- Make a list of must-haves versus nice to haves to prioritize features and avoid overspending.
- How much can you afford? Determine your budget and affordability.

- Vacations: Get the best travel deals by visiting destinations during their off seasons, like Europe in the fall and Mexico in late spring.
- Furniture and appliances: Shop at outlets and discount stores and look for deals in early fall before new models are released.
- Home improvements: Avoid peak periods and find bargains when material inventories are cheaper, such as late fall or winter for outdoor projects and spring or summer for indoor projects.
- Air-conditioning: Install in late winter or early fall, and furnaces in late summer or early spring.
- Designer clothing: Shop for sales at the end of each season and get long-lasting clothes at a fraction of the cost.
- When making big purchases, make sure they match your **core values** and financial goals. Often, people trade in and finance new items just after paying off old ones, which can trap them in endless payments and long-term debt. Before investing a hefty sum, consider if it fits your priorities, and aim for decisions that help build a stable financial future.

## BUYING NEW VERSUS BUYING USED

### The Financial Breakdown *(in Canada)*

GP: "The allure of a brand-new car, with its shine and scent, often comes with a hefty price tag, averaging $740 per month. Alternatively, used cars are more budget-friendly, typically costing around $25,000."

Charles: "They also tend to have lower insurance and registration fees."

GP: "Moreover, new cars can depreciate rapidly, sometimes losing as much as 20% of their value in the first year."

Charles: "When deciding whether to buy a new or used car, we should carefully consider the financial implications."

GP: "Take into account factors like the down payment, monthly payments, and the total cost over the period of ownership. For example, if you're considering a $45,000 car and you have $12,000 from your old vehicle plus $5,000 in savings, you would need a $28,000 loan to cover the remainder. Now, consider your options:

- **Leasing:** With a $5,000 down payment and monthly payments of $434.76 for seven years, your total expenditure during the lease period would be $20,868.48. If you decide to keep the car post-lease, the total cost would be $51,328.28.

- **Buying:** If you opt for purchasing with monthly payments of $618.92, the total expense would be $46,607.55—cheaper than leasing.

- **Waiting and Saving:** If you save $620 monthly for two years, you'll have a $15,000 down payment. Assuming your old car has a trade-in value of $7,000, you'd need to borrow $23,000. This method would result in a total cost of $47,104.02."

Charles: "While the costs of these options seem comparable, it's crucial to remember that our financial journeys are unique, influenced by individual factors and decisions."

GP: "Exactly, by critically evaluating our purchases, we gain control over our finances. We should consider costs thoroughly before buying and avoid impulse shopping to make wiser financial choices."

Charles: "For significant decisions like buying a car, consulting a trusted financial coach can help illuminate your path to financial well-being."

GP: **"Reward yourself when you respect your budget."**

## NUTS AND BOLTS

Before purchasing any big items:

- Consider buying last year's model. You let someone else eat up the depreciation.
- The shorter your payment schedule, the less Money you will pay in interest.
- Determine what is your comfortable monthly payment?
- Remember: What you don't have to pay in interest could go towards fun stuff!
- Never dip into your emergency savings.

DO YOUR HOMEWORK EVERY TIME and find the deal that's waiting for you!

Remember: What you don't have to pay in interest could go toward more fun stuff! (WANTS)

# A LITTLE INSPIRATION

## A Cautionary Tale

Sara and John stopped at a big box store to buy printer ink. On the way to the ink cartridges, they walked by the latest big-screen TV model at 30% off the regular price. It had great sound and HD; they could invite their friends on game night. Instead of meeting their original goal to buy printer ink, they walked out having spent an extra $1,899 (plus tax).

The new TV looked too good in their family room, so they renovated it and turned it into a home theatre. Sara and John figured it was a good investment, as they would spend less Money going out. They installed new lighting, soundproofed the room, installed new flooring, bought a great wireless sound system, and got some new seating to complete the look. Just for fun, they put in an old-style popcorn cart, too. All these purchases were made on credit to be paid later.

John and Sara's original need for a printer cartridge ($50) turned into a spiral of costly wants (over $23,000 plus interest) that they will be paying long after their teenage son has finished university.

> "Modern man drives a dealer-financed car over a bond-financial highway on credit card gas"
>
> – Earl Wilson

CHAPTER 8

# MODERN CHAINS

*"Chains of habit are too light to be felt until they are too heavy to be broken."*
—WARREN BUFFETT

Every day, we find ourselves bombarded with hundreds of advertisements, each trying to convince us that we need a product, even if we've managed just fine without it until now. These advertisers employ sophisticated marketing strategies to entice us to make new purchases. Regrettably, many individuals fall into this trap, which can lead to unwanted debts. While we might maintain appearances of happiness for a while, the weight of accumulating debt can eventually erode our entire way of life.

**ASK YOURSELF:**

- Do I know the total amount of my debts and the interest rates on them?
- Do I only make the minimum payments on my credit cards?

- Could I benefit from a different debt repayment strategy?
- If needed, what would be my debt elimination resolution?

GP strolled into the garage, the cheerful melody of his whistling starkly contrasting the serious discussion on the day's agenda: navigating the tricky terrain of debt. As common as oil stains in a mechanic's life, debt casts a shadow on many lives, necessitating a careful and empathetic approach.

GP: "Unfortunately, many people are captured in the web of debt, struggling to find a way out."

Charles: "Indeed. Despite the abundance of financial wisdom available, debt continues to haunt people like a persistent check engine light."

As they delved deeper into their conversation, GP and Charles illuminated the widespread issue of credit card debt and the role of media and marketing in influencing spending habits, bringing common financial pitfalls into focus.

## CREDIT DANGER SIGNALS

GP: "If you find yourself tempted by the following advertisements, you might be at risk of accumulating excessive debt:

- Don't pay a cent until . . .
- No interest, no payments, for one full year.
- Use your credit card and save 10%.
- Get travel miles for every purchase.

"Look out for these warning signs, buddy! Credit cards and loans can be financial potholes, but if managed wisely, they're valuable tools in a garage— invaluable when inappropriately used."

Charles: "I've been cautious with my credit card, using it for everyday purchases and keeping close tabs on my outgoings through online tracking. My mortgage advisor, Cathie, has advised me that a strong credit history can benefit future home loan negotiations. By being prudent with my credit now, I'm laying the foundation for a secure financial future."

GP: "Credit cards are flexible tools, but they should not be taken lightly. If your spending starts to drift from your budget, it's a signal to steer back on course, just as you would with a car that's off alignment. Remember, a credit card is a financial resource, not a Money tree. Let's return to that financial cheat sheet I gave you—there's always something new to learn in finance."

## GP'S DEBT MANAGEMENT GUIDELINES

- Stick to your budget. Use your credit card for planned expenses and avoid impulsive purchases.
- Avoid interest charges by paying your balance in full each month. Don't buy it if you can't afford to pay it off.
- Use automatic payments. Set up automatic payments to ensure you never miss a payment and avoid late fees.
- Keep track of your spending. Regularly check your credit card statements and watch out for any unusual activity.
- Limit the number of cards. The more credit cards you have, the harder it is to keep track of spending and payments. Stick to one or two cards at most.
- Know your credit limit. Don't max out your credit card; it can harm your credit score. Try to use less than 30% of your available credit.
- Use rewards wisely. If your card offers rewards, use them wisely. Only spend what is necessary to get rewards; ensure any annual fees are worth your rewards.

- Think before making large purchases. A credit card can make it easy to buy now and pay later, but interest charges can quickly add up. Consider if you can afford the purchase before charging it to your card.
- Seek help. If you're struggling with credit card debt, seek help from a licensed financial professional.

Charles: "GP, this handy guide is great. It reminds me of the issue many young people face today. I got my first Mastercard offer at eighteen even before I graduated from university. Students nowadays start their financial journey already saddled with credit card debt."

GP: "Unfortunately, these young people start their career with a chunk of their earnings already earmarked for debt repayment."

Charles: "That is like buying a classic car, only to spend all your time and Money on repairs. The thrill of the ride is lost when you're constantly worrying about the next breakdown."

GP: "There's no joy in working primarily to repay for something you already have. Now let's shift gears and talk about:

## DEBT CONSOLIDATION

GP: "Debt consolidation can be a helpful tool for managing and reducing debt, but it's essential to approach it wisely. Assess your financial situation, research your options, and consider seeking professional advice to determine if debt consolidation aligns with your goals and can lead to improved financial health."

Charles: "Address the root issue, not just the surface-level fixes. If I refine my spending habits, consolidate through refinancing, and use my home's equity, it can be a useful tool rather than just a Band-Aid. It can help with cash flow and even allow for extra mortgage payments. But like any complex repair, it's best to consult an expert—like a mortgage broker."

GP: "Credit and debit cards sure make life easier, but it's easy to lose control if we're not careful. Here's a tip: I keep a note with my credit card, like a maintenance reminder on a car dashboard. It reads:

- Is this a NEED or a WANT?
- Is this expense included in my budget?"

Charles: "What a great idea! I shall give it a try. It will make me think twice before buying something I haven't planned for. But how do we rein in our spending habits? Especially in this digital age where a couple of clicks can lead to a brand-new gadget at our doorstep!"

GP: "Start living on cash! It sounds archaic in this digital world, but the physical act of handling cash can help you stay more conscious of your spending. Remember this great quote from John Dewey: 'No man's credit is as good as his Money.'"

Charles: "For me, smartphones and online tools work better. They track spending, send alerts, and act like a virtual assistant. I admire your old-school methods; they've stood the test of time!"

## THE TOOLBOX TASKS: PAY IT OFF!

GP: "Now, let's talk about the best way to pay it off. Imagine having a credit card balance of $3,675.23. If you don't hit the brakes and pay off the full balance within the grace period of 21 days, you'll find an extra $19.75 tacked onto your ride in interest charges. Now, flip your card over and brace yourself for a shock: if you only make the minimum monthly payment, you'd be on a 30-year and 8-month-long road trip to pay off this card. That's assuming you don't make any detours with additional purchases. It's like buying one car but ending up paying for three! Would you buy three cars when you only need one? I don't think so."

As GP delved into his toolbox, he took out a neatly folded piece of paper and presented it to Charles.

GP: "This, will come handy when advising your clients."

Charles carefully unfolded the paper, revealing GP's four-step debt resolution plan, meticulously penned in his old-fashioned handwriting:

- Keep only two credit cards—the ones with the lowest interest rates. Treat them like spare tires, only for emergencies, by applying the "Vault Technique."

- Move your debt, just like shifting gears. Transfer the balance from high-interest cards to the ones with lower rates. It's a simple tweak, but it could save you a ton in interest, helping you clear your debt faster.

- Handling debt might seem as tough as understanding a car engine's manual. Getting help from a debt consolidation trusty can be useful. They can offer plans, talk to those you owe Money to, and help you become debt-free.

- Embrace the snowball principle. List your debts; start by clearing the smallest one first, then use the freed-up Money to tackle the next.

Charles: "It's like having a service manual for debt! I would also add 'Identify one subscription you can cancel this month to save Money.'

GP: "It's all about the journey, not just the destination. Take it slow, make smart choices, and enjoy the ride to financial liberty."

Charles: "Let me tell you about my recent experience with a client, Josh, a young man enticed by credit cards and instant gratification. Soon, bills piled up, and his joy became a heavy burden. He was determined to change. Following my advice, Josh created a net worth sheet, analyzed his finances, and sold unnecessary items to pay off debts. He learned that jeopardizing tomorrow for today's pleasures was not an option.

He advises others to avoid impulsive spending, analyze their finances, and sell unused possessions to tackle debt. Now, Josh knows that the path to financial freedom requires discipline and sacrifice, and he's also committed to helping others find it."

GP: "And he learned the lesson that today's new toy won't be new tomorrow. Charles, your experience is a cautionary tale that many can relate to. Jumping into the world of credit can be exciting at first. All the gadgets and gizmos are just a swipe away. But when the bills pile up, it feels like you're swapping lunchtime for overtime to feed the bank."

## LET'S PLAY: A MINI QUIZ

GP: "This reminds me of distinguishing between needs and wants, using the debt snowball method to get out of debt."

1. True or false: A 'need' is essential for survival, such as food, shelter, and clothing.
2. Multiple choice: Which of the following is considered a 'want'? a) Rent payment b) Water bill c) Movie tickets d) Health insurance
3. Fill in the blank: In the debt snowball method, you pay off debts from the_____balance to the_____balance.
4. Scenario question: If you have a $500 bonus, which debt do you pay first using the snowball method? a) $450 medical bill, b) $2,000 credit card debt, c) $5,000 student loan.
5. True or false: Buying a luxury watch on sale for your birthday when you have high-interest debt is a financially responsible decision.

*Answers:*

1. *True.*
2. *c) Movie tickets*
3. *Smallest; largest*
4. *a) $450 medical bill. It's the smallest debt.*
5. *False. Even if it's your birthday and might think you deserve this watch it's essential to prioritize debt repayment, especially high-interest debt, over luxury purchases.*

Charles: "This quiz can help players think about the basics of personal finance and debt management in a simplified and interactive way."

GP: "To wrap up the day, here is a good quote from Earl Wilson: 'You want to make 28% returns risk-free? Pay off your credit card.'

> **NUTS AND BOLTS**
>
> **DEBT Formula**: Take control of your debts and credit cards.
> - Find out where that Money goes and put a stop to the leakage.
> - Discipline in your actions
> - Excellence in your attitude
> - Budget all your purchases
> - Time the repayment of your debt
> - Stay focused on your dreams
>
> **Commit to regain control of your life.**
> - If indebtedness overtakes your life, seek professional help to manage your finances.

Charles: "Here's a quick laugh, GP. A guy says, 'I thought I wasn't great with Money, but my credit card company sure loves me—they call every day to say my balance is outstanding'!"

On that note, the buddies ended the day with laughter.

# A LITTLE INSPIRATION

## An Extraordinary Couple

In the city of Coinville, Max had perpetually empty pockets, while Lily's purse mysteriously attracted Money. Coins and bills would leap from Max's hand into Lily's purse whenever they tried to pay for something.

Instead of hoarding their newfound Money, Max and Lily used it for good. They performed magic shows for children, making Money disappear and reappear with Lily's purse. Laughter and applause filled the air.

But Max and Lily realized that the true magic was in helping others. They started a charity, using the Money from Lily's purse to assist those in need.

Max and Lily's story had a profound moral lesson: Money isn't magical; what you do with it matters the most. Their unique ability showed them that using Money to spread happiness, laughter, and kindness was the most enchanting magic.

The couple proved that sometimes the most extraordinary things happen to the most ordinary people, and true magic is found in the goodness of hearts.

CHAPTER 9

# YOUR RELATIONSHIP

"Too many people spend Money they haven't earned to buy things they don't want, to impress people they don't like."
—WILL ROGERS

Talking about Money with your partner can be difficult, especially if you start with different savings and investments. Regardless of how difficult discussing Money with your partner can be, it would be best to have common goals and shared values to ensure a lasting relationship. You may not be aligned on your goals and values at first, but with good discussions, you can understand each other and compromise on important matters. Get and keep your finances in order. Be honest with each other!

**ASK YOURSELF:**

- Do I take time to discuss our financial situation with my partner?

- Am I actively learning about financial management to improve decision-making and investment choices and share knowledge with my partner?
- In what ways can we support and inspire each other's financial growth?

Charles stepped into the garage, dream board in hand, eager to share some fantastic news. It was the perfect time since that day's agenda included a deep dive into understanding Money, uncovering happiness and purpose, and shaping personal values and life goals.

GP: "Discussing Money with your partner might seem a bit awkward. You know, some people are more comfortable talking about sex, politics, or religion than finances. But having conversations about Money is crucial. Honesty is the key; keeping financial secrets can lead to major issues. Always be transparent about your debts, net worth, and investments."

Charles: "You're so right, GP. When Jessie and I got serious and started planning, we saved a significant amount in our tax-free savings account. Plus, we paid off our student loans within the year. Living with our parents and paying modest rent has helped us keep our expenses down for a solid beginning."

GP praised his grandson, who proudly displayed his dream board with his goals and aspirations. They shared a good laugh and profound discussions about his future. Then, Charles reached into GP's toolbox and pulled out GP's manual on managing Money as a couple—a significant bonding moment that reinforced their united financial journey.

## GP'S STEP-BY-STEP GUIDE FOR COUPLES

1. Calculate your combined net worth.
    a. Determine your joint assets and liabilities.
    b. Subtract your debts from your assets to find your net worth.

2. Create a budget together.
    a. Develop a shared budget that outlines your monthly income/expenses.
    b. Allocate specific amounts for essentials, savings, and other spending.
3. Set financial goals.
    a. Discuss your long-term and short-term financial aspirations as a couple.
    b. Define clear and achievable financial goals that you both agree on.
4. Communication is key.
    a. Maintain open and honest communication about your Money matters.
    b. Regularly check in with each other to ensure that you're both on track.
5. Joint or separate accounts.
    a. Decide on common or separate bank accounts or a combination of both.
    b. Determine how you'll manage bills and expenses.
6. Emergency fund.
    a. Establish an emergency fund to cover unexpected expenses.
    b. Aim to save at least three to six months of living expenses.
7. Invest wisely.
    a. Explore investment options and build a diversified portfolio.
8. Plan for retirement.
    a. Start saving for retirement early and take advantage of employer-sponsored plans.
    b. Set retirement goals and regularly review your progress.

9. Review and adjust.
    a. Periodically revisit your budget and financial goals.
    b. Make necessary adjustments based on changing circumstances.
    c. Don't forget to celebrate your wins.
10. Seek professional help.
    a. Consider consulting a financial advisor. They can provide expert guidance tailored to your specific needs.

GP: "Adopting these habits together can lead to better financial health and long-term security. It's important not to impose our financial beliefs on our partners and to engage in open and respectful communication."

Charles: "In relationships, we must be willing to adapt and adjust to understand each other fully. By discovering what brings happiness to both partners, we can create a stronger and more harmonious bond."

In the garage, the talk turned to Money habits while working on Mr. Smith's car. They agreed that old habits, like rusty parts, must be replaced with better ones for good financial health.

GP: "Good Money habits are the engine oil to your financial vehicle, keeping everything running smoothly. Regular saving is a key part of this tune-up."

Charles: "I'm proud to say that my client Josh has finally taken the right turn after driving down a debt-ridden road. He's cruising toward 'Plan, Save, Enjoy!' It's a shift that was much needed. With a clear roadmap and steady pace, he's equipped to enjoy his financial journey and guide others on theirs."

GP: "Absolutely! Mastering Money habits is like learning to drive a stick shift. It takes practice, but you're in full control once you get it.

Plan carefully, and you will have twice as much of your wants!"

Charles: "With solid financial planning, I will go twice as far without the stress of running low. Patience in Money matters is the cruise control of life, ensuring a smooth journey. Armed with this new perspective and my experience in Money matters, I'm enthusiastic about helping others build smart financial habits. My goal is to show them how to manage their Money efficiently to get twice as much with what they earn."

**LET'S PLAY: HAVING TWICE AS MUCH JUST CUTTING OUT PAYING INTEREST**

1. Set aside $300 every month. In 3 months: $300 x 3 = $900.
2. Use $900 for roof repairs in September and cover the additional $600 with a low-interest credit card. Roof cost: $900 + $600 = $1,500.
3. Half of the credit card balance is to be paid before interest kicks in: $600 ÷ 2 = $300. By November, you only owe $300 on the credit card.
4. Continue to save $300 monthly from November to June.
5. In 7 months: $300 x 7 = $2,100.
6. By June, you'll have accumulated $2,100, which is set for the pool.
7. Maintain that $300 monthly discipline from June to the following March.
8. In 9 months: $300 x 9 = $2,700.
9. If the Caribbean trip costs $3,000, then $3,000 − $2,700 = $300 (This balance can be placed on the credit card.)

In our current society, belongings often define us. With this in mind, Charles and GP engaged in a meaningful conversation about true value.

## POSSESSIONS CAN IMPRISON US

Charles: "I'm struggling to guide a client who bases his self-worth on the car he drives. He's always talking about his car despite being married with two kids."

GP: "But can that car return his love? Will it care for him when he is sick or help him during tough times? Remember, true value lies in the love given back. Life is about experiences, not objects."

Charles: "I understand what you're saying. What's more valuable? Buying a $75,000 car or a less expensive one and spending some of that Money on a two-week family holiday to Disneyland?"

## THE CREDIT REPORT JOURNEY

GP compared checking a credit report to a car's health check before a big trip, stressing its importance before making significant financial decisions. Spotting errors on a credit report could hinder progress like a flat tire. Charles agreed, noting the importance of regular financial reviews to avoid setbacks when making significant Money moves.

---

The most used scoring method, the Beacon Score, ranges from 300 to 900. By respecting your repayment and always being ON TIME you can expect better interest rates, especially on larger loans like a mortgage.

**The 5 factors that affect your Credit Score:**

| | |
|---|---|
| Payment History | 35% |
| Utilization | 30% |
| Length – Credit History | 15% |
| Type of Credit | 10% |
| Credit Injuries | 10% |

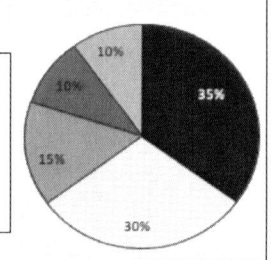

GP: "Credit history is crucial. However, minor setbacks on a credit report are just that—minor. The key to building stellar credit lies in consistently making your payments on time."

Charles: "Because I keep up with bills and use credit wisely, my score takes care of itself. And if things get tricky, I won't hesitate to get some advice."

GP: "Precisely. It's all about those long-term habits."

> **NUTS AND BOLTS**
>
> Discussing Money with your partner can be difficult, but it is crucial and the key to a lasting relationship.
>
> - It would be best if you had common goals and shared values.
> - Mesh your financial goals together to get ahead and reward yourselves when you achieve them.
> - Get and keep your finances in order.
> - Be honest! Keep your word.
>
> Do not worry about your credit score? Just pay your bills on time.
>
> Your financial life begins when you are truly committed to taking charge of Money habits.
>
> Make the changes required now to live a debt-free life.
>
> Get committed. Be ready to take charge.

# A LITTLE INSPIRATION

## Davie's Money Tree

One day, young Davie discovered a rare and extraordinary seed. Excitedly, he shared it with his father, who revealed its magical nature as a Money tree seed. Together, they planted it with care. Intrigued, Davie delved into stories about Money trees and their nurturing requirements. His research unveiled that a Money tree demands diligent attention during the early years and, without that care, it faces slim odds of reaching maturity. Davie dedicated himself to daily visits and regular watering for his baby tree, even though its growth seemed slow and unnoticeable.

Then, after a year, signs of progress emerged. The tree sprouted leaves that astonishingly transformed into dollar bills. Each subsequent year brought forth more leaves, and with unwavering care, the Money tree thrived with lush branches, producing an increasing amount of Money. Eventually, it bloomed into a source of abundance, tending to Davie's needs as long as he nurtured and cared for his cherished tree.

**CHAPTER 10**

# A WEALTHY MINDSET

*"Wealth is not a material gain, but a state of mind."*
—JERRY GILLIES

Money will grow on a tree of perseverance.

Wealthy individuals possess a distinct mindset, not flaunting their wealth through material possessions. Instead, they understand how Money works and how to make it work for them through sound financial management and strategic investments. They follow a well-balanced budget. For them, wealth is not solely about financial success; it's about the freedom to pursue the passions and causes them deeply value. They view Money as a valuable tool to create opportunities and bring positive impact, not only to their lives but also to the lives of others. This approach sets the foundation for their financial success and personal happiness.

**ASK YOURSELF:**

- Do I have a wealthy mindset?
- Do I know what wealthy people have in common?
- Do I have millionaire Money habits?

As GP and Charles busily worked on Mrs. Elliott's car, their conversation turned to the habits and principles of wealthy individuals, exploring what sets them apart and the practices they follow.

GP: "I learned a lot from millionaires' stories. Their Money management is like pruning a tree, cutting away impulsive spending to promote growth. Their smallest savings grow over time."

Charles: "They cut back on unnecessary expenses, which allows them to afford their dreams when the time comes. GP, I know you have a wealthy mind and have been doing this for years."

GP: "You're right! And now, I enjoy the fruits of my investments. We should use our Money like seeds. Nurture it, wait, and invest when the right opportunity comes. That's what wealthy people do."

Charles: "Wealthy people create their fortunes by integrating, saving and investing. They not only have a plan, but also the discipline to stick to their plan."

GP: "The average millionaire has a precise understanding of their financial situation and how their Money is working for them, always."

**WHAT WEALTHY PEOPLE HAVE IN COMMON**

- Typically, live well below their means.
- Use their time, energy, and Money efficiently in ways conducive to wealth-building.
- Prioritize financial independence over displaying high social status.

- Often, they received little to no economic help from their parents.
- Have adult children who tend to be economically self-sufficient.
- Have a knack for identifying lucrative market opportunities.
- Value mentorship and often seek guidance from those more experienced.

GP: "'Being Rich' is about something other than the dollar amount in your bank account. It's about having the time and resources to enjoy what makes you happy."

Charles: You know GP, I agree time is also an important asset class.

## THE RICH MINDSET

GP: "Everyone dreams of being wealthy. The truth is that wealthy people have a certain mindset and apply certain principles that others don't. If you want to be wealthy, apply the same principles as the rich."

Charles: "Surveys show that, unlike the majority who live paycheck to paycheck, millionaires don't always drive new cars, nor do they wear the latest fashions or accessories. Their homes do not always reflect their financial status because they diversify their assets."

GP: "Wealthy people create their fortunes by combining saving and investing. They create a plan and discipline themselves to follow it. The average millionaire always knows exactly how much Money they have and what it's doing. They follow their budget."

Charles: "You are "rich" when you have the time and means to enjoy the activities and people who make you happy. It's a mindset you achieve once your dreams and Money management align."

GP: "We all acknowledge that Money doesn't equal happiness. But deep down, many of us secretly believe it might. We often fail to realize that even if a million dollars suddenly landed in our bank account, if we don't change our old habits—we'd find ourselves just as stressed about Money as before.

**THE ILLUSION OF WEALTH: DANGER SIGNALS**

GP: "Everything we buy has a price tag. Many of us have splurged on an unnecessary item to feel 'rich.' Making this a habit could lead to a financial crash. Some examples of poor spending choices include buying brand-new furniture on credit while your old one is still in pretty good shape, like trading a perfect car for the latest model or buying expensive clothes for 'professional reasons,' while your boss is OK with the regular attire. Another example is always picking up the tab when out with friends, like being the one always filling up the gas tank on a road trip."

Their conversation then veered toward the impact of Money on one's character.

GP: "Anyone aiming to save a million dollars can achieve it; however, the road to riches can sometimes alter our mindset and make us lose sight of who we are."

Charles: "Unfortunately, wealth is often measured by our possessions. It's flattering to have the envy of others, but one day, you will wake up and think—what's my real worth in life?"

GP: "Exactly. Money permits you to experience a better life, but you won't feel accomplished until you have achieved internal peace. Enough will never be enough until you learn to be happy with what you have and can identify the 'what' and 'why' you spend on."

**FROM RAGS TO RICHES**

Charles: "Did you know a $10,000 investment in 1965 in Berkshire Hathaway, an American multinational conglomerate holding company, would be worth over $50 million now? Yet Warren Buffett, the CEO and largest shareholder of that company and one of the wealthiest men alive, lives simply. He has stayed in the same house for 30 years, drives a decade-old car, and enjoys his daily Coke. He also loves to give to charities and helping young people in school understand the principal of Money."

GP: "This shows you can have wealth without letting it change you. Growing up, all I had were the basics. Over time, I aimed to learn from people like Buffett, living simply while investing."

> "Too often, a vast collection of possessions ends up possessing its owner. Besides health, the asset I value most is interesting, diverse, and long-standing friends."
> —Warren Buffett

Charles: "This Buffett quote sounds like Mom: simple, profound, and grounded. It's less about the flashy car and more about the journey!"

## THE FINANCIAL HABITS OF MILLIONAIRES

GP: "Have you ever thought about growing a 'Money tree,' Charles? It's like maintaining a classic car. You invest time and Money, and over time, the value grows, much like a tree sprouting branches."

Charles: "So, it's like regular maintenance tasks, ensuring everything runs smoothly. Regular investments and careful management lead to a fruitful financial future."

GP: "Equip yourself with a wealthy attitude, not just a thick wallet. After all, a true millionaire isn't someone who only has a million dollars but also a million-dollar smile, a million-dollar heart, and most likely a modestly priced, fuel-efficient car.

## NUTS AND BOLTS

Money doesn't alter your character; it merely amplifies what you already are.

The secrets of the rich:

- Borrow Money only when it can generate more in return.
- Ensure the interest they accrue benefits them, not the bank.
- Avoid acquiring possessions merely for the sake of ownership. Otherwise, they may end up possessing you.
- A wealthy mind prizes health and cherishes time with loved ones.

You possess the capacity to think like a millionaire. The choice to do so is entirely yours.

## FINE-TUNING MY FINANCES

- **Buy pre-used.** A used car may have a few miles on it, but it can still rev up in style, minus the hefty price tag!
- **Tame the impulse monster.** Small purchases can inflate quickly. Being vigilant will keep the budget pressure checked!
- **Are you saving before spending?** Are you dreaming of a new set of wheels? Save before you splurge. Nothing drives smoother than a car bought with your saved-up pennies!
- **Pay yourself first.** Automatically route a part of your income towards savings. It's like ensuring that your financial engine never runs out of oil! *It is a crucial step as you are the central figure in your one-of-a-kind journey. Who will attend to your future dreams and desires if you don't?*
- **Discipline is critical.** Resisting the flashing ads is like disregarding the billboards on a highway. Keep your eyes on the road and you're spending in check.
- **Embrace the journey.** Navigating finances can be bumpy, but with a bit of humor and a strong roadmap, you're set for a joyride toward financial happiness!

GP: "Anything is achievable, one step at a time. Taking charge of our destiny and financial liberty is key. That power lies within each of us!

# A LITTLE INSPIRATION

## The Goose with the Golden Eggs

Once upon a time, a farmer found his goose laying eggs of pure, blindingly shiny gold. His eyes lit up like children on Christmas morning each time he found a new golden egg in the nest. Selling these eggs made him richer than he'd ever dreamed. Soon, his dreams became more prominent, and his patience got smaller. His greed overtook him, and he thought, why wait for one egg a day when I could have them all at once? So, in a fit of greed, he decided to perform impromptu surgery on the poor goose, expecting a gold mine inside. But alas, no gold! Just regular old goose innards. Having killed his golden goose, his dreams of riches crumbled.

CHAPTER 11

# THE GOLDEN RULES

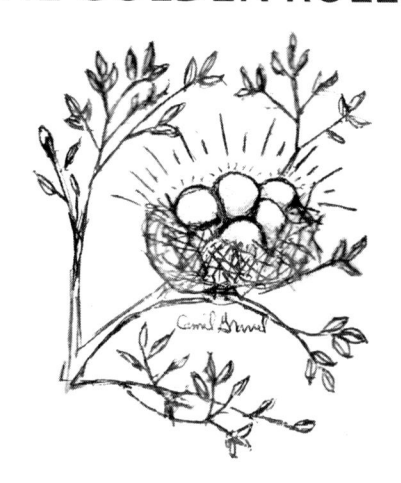

"We live by the Golden Rule.
Those who have the gold make the rules."
—BUZZIE BAVASI

Just as the fastest car doesn't always win the race, becoming wealthy rarely comes from your salary alone. Instead, it's about pacing yourself, filling up your financial tank first every payday, and letting compound interest (the turbo boost of finance) power you down the track to your long-term goals. There's no need to be a mechanical genius—keep your financial engine well-oiled by prioritizing yourself on payday. The horsepower of compound interest and investment returns will do the heavy lifting for you while you get to watch your financial journey speed into the fast lane. That's a pit crew's secret Money rule!

**ASK YOURSELF:**

- Is my Money currently working for me or against me?
- Am I effectively managing my expenses to maximize my financial growth?
- Am I taking advantage of the power of my financial tools and compounding interest and returns?

Charles enters the family garage with a poster full of pictures, excited for his next lesson on the "Golden Rules." The idea sounded intriguing—one doesn't need to be a financial mechanic to build wealth. Charles and Jessie understood that on this journey, they were not only drivers but also the highest-paid employees.

## THE GOLDEN RULE

GP: "Charles, we've mapped out our financial route, tuned the budget and saved a few extra dollars. Staying consistent with investing and allowing compound interest to do the heavy lifting is key."

Charles: "Now, it's time for the fun part—**spending.**"

GP: "And it all starts with the 'Golden Rule.'"

Charles: "Ah, the 'pay yourself first' principle. It's like checking the oil and filling up the tank before embarking on a road trip."

> The Golden Rule: pay yourself first.
> Fuel up your financial future before hitting
> the road of spending.

GP: "Absolutely. As discussed, when we set up our budget, the first payee should always be YOU. Ideally, 10% should go straight into your financial maintenance fund. But if you're new to this and the gears feel stiff, start with just 2%. Then, shift up another 2% every few months until you reach that 10%. And before you know it, you'll be cruising in the fast lane to financial freedom!"

## WHY SHOULD YOU BE THE FIRST PAYEE?

Charles: "In my financial plan, 'pay yourself first' is like to the safety principle in a car: secure your stability first. By directing the initial portion of my income to savings, I lay the groundwork for enduring financial health, ensuring I can assist others without jeopardizing my financial well-being."

GP: "Exactly, son. Saving first is self-care. It's like putting on your seatbelt before starting the car. This proactive step means you're ready for the future, demonstrating self-respect. You'll secure a solid financial stance and earn others' respect. Now, let's talk about the power of numbers."

## THE POWER OF COMPOUND GROWTH

Charles: "Imagine a world where every dollar you save works as hard as you do. That's the magic of compound interest. It's like turbocharging your savings."

GP: "Correct, it's kind of a performance booster for our financial engines, but remember, the key to maximizing this turbocharged performance is to fuel your financial vehicle consistently."

Charles: "They taught us in school this mind-boggling formula to understand compound interest: **A = P(1 + r/n)^(nt)**. It felt like trying to assemble an engine without a manual. But if I break it down, it's like the parts of a car:

$$A = P(1 + \frac{r}{n})^{nt}$$

- ▸ 'A' is the shiny, upgraded model we want for our old clunker.
- ▸ 'P' is the principal amount to transform it.
- ▸ 'r' is the fuel efficiency or annual interest rate.
- ▸ 'n' is the number of pits stops or times that interest is compounded per year.
- ▸ 't' is the duration of our journey in years.

Charles: Let's say I hit the road with $1,000 in my pocket and a map leading to a treasure chest yielding a 5% interest compounded annually. After five years, I'd find myself with $1276.28! That's the actual horsepower of compound interest."

GP: "Well, well, Charles, you've not just assembled the engine but also turbocharged it! Compound interest is indeed the powerhouse driving the car of wealth. And the best part? Unlike us drivers, it never needs to take a break."

Charles: "Yep! And as you know, this is because with compound interest, the amount grows based on the initial principal and the accumulated interest. It's like a snowball rolling downhill, gathering more snow (interest). The bigger the snowball gets, the more snow it picks up on every turn."

GP: "Let's break down the above $1,000. You invest $1,000 at an interest rate of 5% compounded annually. After the first year, you'll earn $50 in interest (5% of $1,000). So, your total becomes $1,050."

Charles: "The magic begins in the second year. You don't earn interest only on your initial $1,000; you earn it on the new total of $1,050. This means you'll earn $52.50 in interest in the second year, bringing your total to $1,102.50."

GP: "And it continues this way, with your interest earnings growing yearly. This is why it's often said that the earlier you start investing, the better. The longer your Money compounds, the faster it grows."

Charles: "For those aiming to amass wealth, understanding and harnessing the power of compound interest is crucial. It's not about how much you start with but how long you let it grow and at what rate."

GP: "Correct! The key is patience, persistence, and letting time do its magic. Remember, the most powerful factor in compounding is time. Start early, and even small investments can lead to significant gains."

Charles: "With this tool in my financial toolkit, the road to wealth becomes not just a possibility but a probability. The journey might be extended, but with compound interest in the driver's seat, I'm in for a smooth and accelerating ride!

GP: "Now I've got a game for us to play."

---

### THE POWER OF NUMBERS!

Peggy and Henry had different views on savings. Peggy, at 25, invested $50 each month at 8% interest for 40 years.

Henry waited 20 years until he was 45 to begin investing $100 at the same rate as Peggy for the next 20 years. (He invested double Peggy's amount for half the time that she did.)

They both invest the **same** amount of $24,000.

**Let's review their investments results**

| | |
|---|---|
| at 65, Peggy has | 174,550.39 |
| at 65, Henry has | 58,902.04 |
| **Difference:** | **115,648.35** |

When Henry invested his first $100, Peggy had already accumulated $29,451.02. To achieve the same result at 65, Henry would have had to invest $296.34 each month for 20 years, almost six times as much as Peggy put in each month. Imagine, $300 versus $50! This is **the magic of compound interest**.

**This gives real meaning to 'Time is Money.'**

> "Compound interest is the eighth wonder of the world."
> —Albert Einstein

Charles and GP had a riot playing their financial games, their laughter echoing throughout the garage. But GP wasn't done yet.

GP: "Talking about this magic of the power of numbers with you reminds me of a good one. Although the Canadian penny is no longer in circulation, this old cliché is one of my favorites, and I still apply today. Consider this: get paid $10,000 for 30 days of work, or one penny on the first day, doubled each day for the same 30 days? What's your pick?"

Charles: "The $10,000, of course. A penny can't be worth that much in only 30 days!

GP: "Wrong answer, son. If you picked the penny, you'd walk away from your 30-day job with over $5 million!"

**LET'S PLAY: THE PENNY PARADOX**

| Day | Pay | Day | Pay |
| --- | --- | --- | --- |
| 1 | $0.01 | 16 | $327.68 |
| 2 | $0.02 | 17 | $655.36 |
| 3 | $0.04 | 18 | $1,310.72 |
| 4 | $0.08 | 19 | $2,621.44 |
| 5 | $0.16 | 20 | $5,242.88 |
| 6 | $0.32 | 21 | $10,485.76 |
| 7 | $0.64 | 22 | $20,971.52 |
| 8 | $1.28 | 23 | $41,943.04 |
| 9 | $2.56 | 24 | $83,886.08 |
| 10 | $5.12 | 25 | $167,772.16 |
| 11 | $10.24 | 26 | $335,544.32 |

| 12 | $20.48 | 27 | $671,088.64 |
| 13 | $40.96 | 28 | $1,342,177.28 |
| 14 | $81.92 | 29 | $2,684,354.56 |
| 15 | $163.84 | 30 | **$5,368,709.12** |

## THE GOLDEN RULES

In a quaint town nestled between rolling hills and whispering rivers, young Alex faced a peculiar dilemma. He was offered a summer job at the old mill. The owner, Mr. Hawthorne, posed an unusual payment plan: "Take $10,000 for the season's toil, or embark on a journey with me where a penny today could be a fortune tomorrow."

Alex, intrigued yet skeptical, chose the adventure of the penny. Alex's skepticism waned daily as the penny doubled, and wonder took place. By the end of the first week, the amount was barely enough for a meal. Friends laughed, but Alex held onto Mr. Hawthorne's cryptic smile when he'd posed the offer.

As weeks unfolded, the power of growth began to show. The sum wasn't just doubling but reshaping Alex's understanding of Money. Neighbors started to whisper, the laughter turned into awe, and Alex's anticipation grew with the burgeoning sum.

On the thirtieth day, the entire town gathered as Alex received the final sum, a testament to patience and the magic of compound interest. It wasn't just about Money; it was about foresight, starting small and growing beyond imagination. It was $5,368,709.12, which echoed through the hills, rivers, and hearts, forever changing the town's perspective on "just a penny."

And so, Alex's financial journey began, not with a hefty check, but with a simple cent. A lesson in saving and the wisdom of Mr. Hawthorne's investment insights.

Charles: "Unbelievable! I should start brushing up on my math skills, huh? This is such a powerful example to share with my clients. Unfortunately, many people don't take the time to understand or apply this incredible power of compounding."

GP: "You're right. The beauty of numbers can be overwhelming to some people, especially when it's related to finance. But as you've seen, it doesn't seem so intimidating anymore when simplified like we did today. On another note, are you familiar with the Rule of 72?"

Charles: "Absolutely, GP. It's a handy tool that helps you estimate when your Money will double based on your interest rate. Think of it as your financial journey's speedometer."

GP: "With these financial tools at our disposal—compound interest, the Golden Rule, and the Rule of 72—we've got ourselves a high-performance race car on the road to financial freedom! How about we crunch some numbers together, just for fun?"

Charles: "Okay!"

GP: "Let's say you open an investment account with $1,000, with earns an annual rate of 5% interest. Here's how the Rule of 72 works: you divide 72 by the interest rate, which is 5% (72 ÷ 5 = 14.4). This means it will take 14.4 years for your initial $1,000 to double $2,000. Now, imagine if your investment earned 10% annually; your Money would double in just 7.2 years!"

Charles: "The beauty lies in the magic of compound interest. The key is setting aside a certain percentage of your income."

GP: "The secret is for every dollar that falls into your hands, set aside 10% from day one."

Charles: "Ten percent is a goal, not a mandate. If you can't manage that now, start with a smaller amount, even 2%, if that's what's feasible. The most important thing is to establish this new habit."

GP: "Aim to increase your savings by 2% each year until you reach that 10% goal by the fifth year."

Charles: "This strategy, known as progressive saving, will encourage you to either increase your income or decrease your expenses. What matters the most is to start paying yourself first, **prioritizing saving before spending.**"

GP: "When it comes to managing Money, there's one rule that I already talked to you about that you should hold above all others: the Golden Rule. As mentioned, it's quite simple: you should always be the number one payee. You work hard for your Money; you are the first person who should benefit from it. Then make your Money fruitful—invest wisely."

---

**NUTS AND BOLTS**

The Golden Rule: the number one payee is YOU.

Pay yourself first, above all, and ALWAYS!

Compound interest is interest earned from reinvesting the interest.

Start at 20 years old, if you can. Contribute $100/month at 10% and by age 65, you will have $1,000,000.

Remember, it's the little commitments you make regularly that can give you the greatest results.

The Golden Rule + Compound Magic = FINANCIAL FREEDOM

# A LITTLE INSPIRATION

## The Miser and His Gold

Once, there was a miser who loved his hidden gold pot more than anything else. He'd visit his hidden treasure frequently, only under the cover of night. A sneaky neighbor, however, noticed his strange outings. One day, in the miser's absence, he stole the gold.

When the miser discovered his loss, he was devastated. His cries caught the attention of a passerby, who asked him why he was so upset. The miser explained his loss, but when the passerby asked why he hadn't kept the gold at home, the miser was shocked. "Use it? I never planned to use it!"

The passerby laughed and suggested, "Why don't you just bury a rock in its place? It will serve the same purpose!"

The story reminds us that Money is only valuable if it's spent or invested wisely, not hoarded away. Remember the old saying: "You can't take it with you!" if you don't want to end up acting stingy like a miser. The most famous fictional miser is probably Scrooge in Dickens *A Christmas Carol*.

CHAPTER 12

# GIVE YOUR MONEY A JOB

*"How many millionaires do you know who have become wealthy by investing in savings accounts? I rest my case."*
—ROBERT G. ALLEN

Give your Money a job! is a wise philosophy. Saving establishes a financial foundation while investing ensures your Money actively grows. Like assigning roles to employees, give your Money a purpose through strategic investments. This way your Money will work tirelessly to help realize your financial goals.

**ASK YOURSELF:**

- Am I educating myself about my finances and investments?
- Who is my trusted financial advisor?
- Have I taken advantage of tax benefits: tax-free savings account

(TFSA), registered retirement savings plan (RRSP), and first home savings account (FHSA)?
- ▸ Have I reviewed my taxes with a tax specialist for any additional credit?
- ▸ Do my investments align with my goals.

Now, Charles was not just a car enthusiast but also a financial guide, leading clients to prosperity. With its rich aroma of motor oil and echoes of GP's laughter, the garage remained his sanctuary. The two buddies engaged in meaningful dialogue about financial well-being here, surrounded by the sounds of tools and the wisdom in the air.

GP: "**Saving** means setting aside income for immediate needs or wants. It sounds straightforward, but the temptation to spend can often outweigh the discipline to save."

Charles: "It's like the old saying about oxygen masks on a plane—we must secure ours before helping others."

GP: "Employing your Money means adopting an active role in your financial health. Saving builds a foundation; investing puts your Money in motion to grow. Think of yourself as the CEO of your finances, assigning every dollar a role, ensuring each contributes to your long-term goals."

Charles: "**Investing,** on the other hand, simply means allocating your Money to generate returns. I always tell my clients that the investments chosen should be based on their risk tolerance and time horizon. If you want to turbocharge your portfolio, ensure you have the right professional who cares!"

GP: "Exactly. It's about utilizing the power of your Money to the fullest, allowing compound interest to expand its worth progressively. That's the real magic in growing wealth."

## INVESTMENTS IN DREAMYVILLE

GP: "Charles, you've been quite the financial enthusiast lately. Money in Dreamyville isn't just any worker; it's the VIP of the tireless dollar corporation. Always on the move, working round the clock."

Charles: "You're right. Thanks to our strategies, every dollar I have plays a significant role, just like a well-coordinated pit crew. It's about ensuring every dollar is actively engaged, either racing on the track or being refueled and maintained for the next lap."

GP: "You know, Uncle Benny never tapped into the potential of his Money. He kept it parked, missing out on all the exhilarating race of investments."

Charles: "Indeed. To diversify, Money needs to be dynamic, allocating funds to short-term and long-term investments. It's like having sprint racers and marathon runners in its team, each contributing to the overall victory."

GP: "And Money ensures that its crew of dollar 'racers' are performing at their peak."

Charles: "With continuous tuning and maintenance. Just as a race car needs regular check-ups, I frequently review my portfolio. It helps me identify where Money's investments crew is giving me the best mileage, which needs more tweaking. Today's financial tools and apps make tracking performance so much easier."

GP: "Ah, the beauty of technology! It's like having an onboard diagnostics system for your car. Tell me, Charles, how do you fuel these racers? Where does savings come into play?"

Charles: "Well, let's compare saving to the high-octane fuel that powers the engines. As the first Payee, I ensure that 8% to 10% of my income goes directly into savings. This serves as a reserve for pit stops and allows me to be ready to pounce on lucrative investment opportunities when they arise."

GP: "You must have had a good mentor. You truly embraced the essence of making your dollar crew work with you and for you. But, as we know, every race has its challenges. How do you handle the curves and bumps on the financial track?"

Charles: "Risk management, GP. As a racer wears protective gear, I have insurance and emergency funds. They act as my financial safety nets. Plus, staying informed and updated about market trends is like understanding the track conditions before a race."

GP: "Wise words. You're not just racing; you're aiming for the championship. With such an approach, Dreamyville's financial Grand Prix has a promising candidate."

Charles: "Thanks. With the right mindset, tools, and guidance, anyone can optimize their Money crew and take the pole position in their financial race. Building an investment portfolio is like tuning a car engine. We've got:

- High-interest savings and GICs: our trusty family sedan.
- Stocks and bonds: the fuel-efficient hybrid.
- Mutual and segregated funds: the high-performance sports car."

GP: "Some folks even venture into alternative investments like cryptocurrencies. Quite the cross-country trip in a self-driving electric car!"

Charles: "That's true, but higher speeds come with higher risks. A good financial plan isn't a reckless joyride; it's a well-planned road trip. We need an emergency fund, our spare tire. As you taught me, starting to save early has been a turbo boost for our financial journey."

GP: "A good financial planner is your GPS, guiding you toward your financial destinations. Savings fuel your short-term trips, while investments keep you moving on long journeys, like your retirement."

Charles: "Thanks to your advice, GP, and Cathie's guidance, Jessie and I are in the driver's seat. We've invested our TFSA into fuel-efficient

GICs and high-interest savings. We're tuning up our portfolio with low-risk investment funds. Our dream ride—our new home—is just over the horizon."

GP: "Wow, Charles I am impressed!"

## THE PIT STOP OF REGISTERED SAVINGS ACCOUNTS

Charles: "A car engine won't do much good without wheels, much like my high-interest savings account wouldn't be much use without some stocks, bonds, and mutual funds for balanced growth. Self-driving cars must be well tested beforehand to avoid bad financial accidents."

GP: "Exactly! While Money can't buy happiness, it can surely upgrade our ride or offer us a nice box of chocolates. Now, what's your take on RRSPs and TFSAs, both Canadian tax-advantaged accounts for saving and investing?"

Charles: "RRSPs are like classic cars, aging gracefully into a retirement beauty, while TFSAs are like electric cars—zipping tax-free, leaving the taxman choking on dust!"

GP: "I learned from Cathie this week that there is a new plan on our radar to help speed up the route to savings and home ownership. Tell me about it."

Charles: "It is called the first home savings account (FHSA). We can save up to $40,000 toward our first home. Contributions are tax deductible and not taxable when you withdraw them, just like withdrawing under the RRSP Home Buyers' Plan."

GP: "Does this replace the Home Buyers' Plan?"

Charles: "Nope. It is in addition to the Home Buyers' Plan. So, between both plans, first-time buyers can save up to $100,000 as a down payment. And remember, the entire amount is also a tax deduction!"

GP: "Wow! This is a powerful savings engine to help first-time home buyers reach their destination faster!"

> ### LET'S PLAY: THE SAVINGS GAME
>
> GP: "Picture this: you're making $50,000 annually. Now, if you decide to pack a lunch instead of eating out, you're saving $15 every day. Over a year, that adds up to $3,900. It's as if you've given yourself a 7.8% salary increase without asking your boss.
>
>> **The RRSP route.** Turning to RRSP contributions, let's say you're in the 40% tax bracket. Here's where it gets interesting: $3,900 saved could translate into a $1,560 tax refund.
>>
>> **Dual advantages of RRSP and TFSA.** Investing in RRSPs and TFSAs is like owning a car with two engines; you benefit now and later. With RRSPs, you score an instant tax break, potentially dropping to a lower tax tier that enhances your purchasing power for life's milestones or simply fueling your retirement dreams. It's comparable to trading in a thirsty old clunker for a sleek, fuel-efficient machine.
>>
>> **TFSA's power surge.** Think of TFSAs as your financial nitro boost. They shield your investment growth from taxes and allow you to tap into your funds at any moment—ideal for those financial detours—without the tax tolls."
>
> Charles: "It's just like being behind the wheel. With RRSPs and TFSAs, you must be aware of your contribution limits—stick to the speed limit to avoid unnecessary fines and penalties on your financial highway!"

## TFSA versus RRSP

GP: "Now, this is something so many have difficulty getting their head around. Which one is best: TFSA or RRSP?

Charles: "It is like buying a car, GP—you need to research before you sign on the dotted line. Both are tax-sheltered, and both can hold the same type of investments, BUT, if someone needs to reduce their taxes and or get a tax refund, RRSPs will give you a bigger bang for your buck! But when in doubt, seek help."

## RESPs and RDSPs

Registered Education Savings Plan (RESP) and Registered Disability Savings Plan (RDSP) are Canadian investment accounts designed for specific saving purposes.

Charles: "RESP is a savings account for parents who want to save for their children's post-secondary education. The contributions grow tax-free until the beneficiary is ready to go to college or university. The Canadian government can add to these savings through the Canada Education Savings Grant and other programs."

GP: "RDSP is intended to help individuals with disabilities and their families save for long-term financial security. The contributions are not tax-deductible, but the investment growth is tax-deferred. The government offers with bonds and grants, which can significantly enhance the savings in the RDSP."

Charles: "Now that it's time for Jessie and I to have kids, an RESP will be like handing over the keys to their academic future—a sweet sixteen gift! And RDSPs? They're like a minivan with all the comfort features for people with disabilities."

GP: "Let's not forget that on this financial journey, you're not just the driver but also the mechanic. Keep your eyes on the road and watch out for those financial potholes!"

Charles: "Investing isn't a race; it's a steady drive. The best time to invest was yesterday, the second-best time is now. It's less about instant acceleration and more about cruise control. Money has to be at its best."

GP: "We must keep a steady hand and avoid sudden jerks on the steering wheel when the markets fluctuate."

Charles: "You're right, GP. We can't control market speed bumps, but we can control how we steer over them. Regular portfolio pit stops and adjustments are a must to keep us on track towards our financial destination."

GP: "Every investor has their own ride, with unique goals, risk tolerances, and timelines. So, it's important to have a financial advisor as a knowledgeable companion who helps navigate through the complexities of investing."

The garage was more than just a hub of mechanical tinkering. It was a crucible for priceless financial wisdom!

> **NOTE:** Canada's Tax-Free Savings Accounts are exemplary models for other countries. These accounts showcase effective financial planning tools that could inspire similar savings strategies globally.

## MULTIPLE STREAMS OF INCOME CHOICES

GP: "Charles, have you ever tried to rev up a hill with a single-cylinder engine?"

Charles: "Not really, but I imagine it'd be like driving with the parking brake on?"

GP: "Exactly! Now, picture that one-cylinder engine as your sole income stream. It can be slow and may not always bring you where you want to be, especially when financial uphill battles come your way."

Charles: "So, you're suggesting that having multiple income streams is like switching to a beefy V8 engine that provides the horsepower needed to race up life's fiscal inclines?"

GP: "That's the spirit! More income streams mean more financial flexibility! Who wouldn't want a financial engine that roars with possibilities? Imagine if your car could run on gasoline, electricity, and solar power!"

Charles: "Sounds like an eco-friendly speed demon!"

GP: "Consider those diverse fuels as different income streams. Gasoline is your full-time job, a reliable fuel that keeps your financial engine humming. Electricity symbolizes side job—not as constant as gasoline but an extra push when needed."

Charles: "Cool, and the solar power?"

GP: "Ah, that's the sweet spot: passive income. Think dividends from stocks, rental income, royalties, or income from a side business. It quietly fills your financial battery, even when you're off the clock, much like the sun charges a solar car."

Charles: "I see. By balancing these different 'fuels,' we can create a robust and efficient financial vehicle. One may not work in all conditions, but collectively, they'll cruise through any fiscal landscape!"

GP: "You've hit the nail on the head, Charles! Regarding income, remember my old man's car wisdom: 'Don't put all your fuel in one tank!'"

## THE TAX COLLECTOR

GP: "In many countries, a significant portion of your income goes towards taxes, sometimes lasting until mid-year. This happens regardless of whether you're on payroll or self-employed. Understandably, people search for legal avenues to retain more earnings."

Charles: "There are many legal avenues to save on tax. Tax deductions and credits are among the primary methods. Always keep your receipts and consult your local tax guidelines. In Canada, for instance, the CRA website provides extensive information."

GP: "Indeed, many governments provide measures to minimize taxes. Here are some commonly overlooked tax deductions:

- Contributions to RRSPs or FHSA's retirement savings plans
- Union and professional dues
- Investment counsel fees
- Carrying charges and interest expenses for non-registered investments
- Childcare and employment expenses
- Capital loss deductions
- Security options deductions
- Pension splitting

Charles: "You're right, GP. Timely tax filings are also pivotal. They're not just about avoiding penalties but ensuring you receive all due credits, and they're important when applying for loans. Moreover, your taxes must be filed promptly to access federal and provincial credits, like child tax benefits or GST credits."

GP: "I agree. While tax season might not be everyone's favorite, diligence can lead to substantial savings. Think of it as routine car maintenance: it might be a hassle, but it ensures everything runs efficiently."

## BATTLING INFLATION

Charles: "Have you noticed how costs keep rising over the years?"

GP: "Absolutely. It's like consistently pumping air into a tire, watching it expand. We refer to that phenomenon as inflation!"

Charles: "I love that analogy. Inflation means the general price level for goods and services increases, so our Money doesn't stretch as far as it once did."

GP: "And just as a tire that loses air affects a car's performance, inflation reduces the buying power of our Money. It's vital to include inflation into our financial strategies."

Charles: "Makes sense. To keep pace with inflation, we need our Money to grow at a rate that outstrips it. This might involve diversifying into investments, GICs, or high-interest savings accounts."

GP: "By including inflation, in the big picture, we ensure our Money maintains its value, paving the way for a stable financial future."

## SHIFTING GEARS TO BUSINESS OWNERSHIP

GP: "Charles, starting a business could turbocharge your financial journey. It's like adding an extra gear to your car for better performance. More income streams from a business can boost your financial growth and bring tax benefits. But just like you'd check your car before hitting the gas, ensure you do your homework before launching a business."

Charles: "Interesting that you bring that up. Apart from my role as a financial advisor, I've been pondering about expanding our garage business. I've done my due diligence: assessing the market, studying our competitors, weighing the costs, and sketching a business plan. Anything else I should have on my checklist?"

GP: "Taking a moment to reflect is always wise! Make sure you assemble the right 'support crew,' like an accountant, attorney, and business consultant, to guide your path. Their expertise can help confirm you're moving in the right direction."

Charles: "What about steering through start-up pitfalls?"

GP: "Starting a business holds great potential but demands attention and effort, particularly in the beginning. Think of it this way: owning a business is like driving a high-performance sports car. It offers exhilaration and can speed up your journey, but you must stay vigilant about maintenance. If you don't check the fuel gauge, you might end up stranded. Likewise, many start-ups stall within the first five years because they miss essential financial checks."

Charles: "It's easy for an entrepreneur to get so passionate about their product or service that the vital side of financial management is neglected."

GP: "Exactly! Just as a car relies on fuel, a business depends on consistent cash flow. You might be excellent at your trade, but it's like pushing that sports car on fumes if you're not attentive to your business's financial pulse."

Charles: "Be it cars or finances, thorough research and a trustworthy team ensure the journey remains smooth and efficient!

## TRANSITIONING INTO EMERGENCY FUNDS

GP: "As we've navigated these financial roads together, we've covered some ground. We've talked about investments, multiple income streams, and tax savings. But let's remember one essential element: the emergency fund. You know how we always keep a spare tire in the trunk?"

Charles: "Of course, that's Emergency Preparedness 101 in car ownership."

GP: "Exactly. Now, let's consider your emergency funds as your financial spare tire. Just like a spare tire covers you in times of an unexpected flat, an emergency fund helps in unforeseen financial situations. A robust emergency fund should cover three to six months of your gross salary."

Charles: "I've crunched the numbers, and our TFSA serves as our financial 'jack and wrench,' equipped to handle unexpected financial hiccups like a sudden job loss, an illness, or a major repair."

GP: "There's plenty more road to travel on this financial journey."

Charles: "Great! I'm excited to keep learning and put these lessons into practice."

GP: "That's the spirit! Remember, keep your hands steady on the financial wheel and your eyes on the road ahead. Next up, we'll dive into a new topic. But for now, let's take a break, grab a soda, and revel in the knowledge we've gained today. I'm proud you took the time to learn new tricks that you can share with your clients!

Charles: "Absolutely! And an emergency fund is so important! It's not just a buffer but the financial equivalent of a life jacket in a sea of uncertainty. The peace of mind keeps you afloat during life's unexpected storms.

GP: "Learn to put your Money to work to increase its value. Assign each dollar a role in your financial adventure."

Charles: "Savings are your vehicle's sturdy frame, essential for the journey, while investments are the powerful engine propelling you forward. Together, they transport you toward your aspirations. So, fuel up with savings, shift gears with investments, and steer your financial path purposefully. Every dollar working for you brings you closer to your destination of prosperity."

## NUTS AND BOLTS

Many people don't realize the advantages of putting Money into an RRSP or a TFSA.

You can reap some of the benefits now!

- For RRSPs, you defer paying taxes (until you are in a lower income bracket when you can withdraw it).
- Your RRSP contributions are tax deductible and may put you into a lower tax bracket, in which case you will pay even less tax.
- With TFSAs, you can eliminate taxes on investment gains and access the funds to short-term changes in your plan.
- Remember, a financial plan is never a gamble.

A good plan only partially relies on the growth of one type of asset.

As part of creating a life without financial worry, make the following commitment to yourself:

This year, thanks to my financial management plan, I will:

Build my emergency fund to_____

I will deposit_____ in my RRSPs or TFSA.

*Rule No.1: Never lose money.*
*Rule No.2: Never forget rule No.1."*
**WARREN BUFFETT**

**To win at the Money Game**

Manifest abundance by optimizing your financial strategy.

- **M** aximize your income through smart career choices.
- **O** bserve and learn from the financial habits of the successful.
- **N** avigate the markets with diligence and patience.
- **E** mpower your future with a diverse portfolio.
- **Y** ield to wisdom, not whims, in your financial journey.

## A LITTLE INSPIRATION

### Cathie's Story

Success in real estate starts with the belief and mindset that you have what it takes to put the funds in place, work hard to fill in the gaps for funds needed and fulfill the lender's requirements. Cathie started investing in real estate in 1989, buying her first house at 19. Cathie was working as a waitress at the time, and after moving into a poor area of the city, in a cockroach-infested building, she was motivated to move out as fast as possible. She kept her costs low, worked six days a week and 12-hour shifts, and saved the 10% needed to buy a house over the next eight months. As she was a waitress with fluctuating hours, her dad was able to be a guarantor for the first year to help her qualify, and she got the keys to her first home. As she went back to school the following year, she was able to rent out rooms to other students to help pay the mortgage and thus graduate from college.

She and her husband now have more than forty properties ranging from townhomes and multi-units to a commercial building, and they are working on a small residential development.

It all starts with finding your passion, keeping your mindset in check, and surrounding yourself with mentors and like-minded people to journey with.

Yes, you can buy a home. You can purchase many properties if that is what you also dream about! Success depends on your support system!

CHAPTER 13

# GETTING AHEAD IN REAL ESTATE

*"Success in real estate starts when you believe you are worthy of it."*
—MICHAEL FERRARA

The true measure of life extends beyond the price tag of a house or the sum of one's wealth. It's about the fulfillment found in how we spend our time, manage our finances, and utilize our abilities to enrich our lives and the lives of those around us. A home is more than just a valuable asset for a family; it stands as a testament to stability and progress. With strategic financial planning and savvy real estate investment, owning a home becomes an attainable milestone. It also becomes a means to potentially build equity, leverage wealth, and secure a financial advantage for the future. It's not just about getting ahead; it's about laying a foundation for prosperity that can last generations.

**ASK YOURSELF:**

- What are my real estate dreams and goals?

- Do I have a trusted mortgage agent?
- Is a rental property on my radar?

Charles loved visiting GP's garage, where he'd refuel on financial wisdom and fine-tune his Money management skills. Their discussions often revolved around investments, tax strategies, and, recently, the intricacies of real estate.

## NAVIGATING THE REAL ESTATE HIGHWAY

Charles: "Preparing for a home purchase while home prices are skyrocketing is quite the journey."

GP: "Remember my first house? It cost me $36,000, and it felt like a fortune back then. Yet it was an investment worth every penny."

Charles: "In today's market, that's the price of a used car!"

GP: "True! But don't fixate on the cost of the home; think of its potential value over time. A home isn't just shelter; it's more like a long-term investment."

Charles: "Venturing into the housing market feels like navigating an intricate maze. But Jessie and I are ready for a new, bigger home! We've set a budget and are prepared, but navigating the mortgage process feels like driving through a dense fog!"

GP: "Keep your 'emergency kit' handy—financial surprises can pop up anytime! And remember, don't stretch your finances too thin."

Charles: "Right. We're inspecting before buying to ensure we avoid any hidden Money pits. I remember your advice, GP, when we bought our first house. To help pay off the mortgage quicker, Dad renovated the basement into a rental unit. That was a good move."

GP: "Let's review those important steps when buying a first house!"

## HOME BUYING STEPS: NAVIGATING WITH EXPERTS

**Down payment strategy.** Calculate what you can afford for your down payment.

**Savvy savings transfer.** If your savings are in a TFSA, consider moving them to an RRSP before the tax season to reap some tax benefits. Discuss the Home Buyers' Plan with your mortgage agent and remember the funds should stay in the RRSP for at least 90 days.

**Be prepared.** Before you get the green light:

- Gather documents. Assemble all the necessary financial documents.
- Find a professional partnership. Work with a reputable mortgage agent or broker well in advance—aim for three months out.

**Secure pre-approval** when approval is in sight.

**After you're approved.**

- Review the contract. Go over the purchase agreement carefully.
- Update finances. Keep your financial documents updated and on hand.
- Ensure you understand all your mortgage terms once you've received the final approval.
- Set aside funds for closing costs, typically around 3.5% of the home's value.

**Choose your real estate co-pilot.**

- Get to know the housing market you're entering.
- Start your search for the perfect home.
- Have an emergency fund for those just-in-case moments.

Charles: "GP, it's important to secure a solid down payment and ensure to show at least a 90-day history of these funds to the mortgage agent. It's also wise to avoid stretching your finances too thin. I always advise my clients not to borrow the maximum amount offered, since rainy days can happen."

**Additional Tips:**

- Down payment: Safely invest to avoid risk; consider an FHSA to accelerate it.
- Pre-approval: Avoid borrowing the maximum amount.
- Home search checklist: Focus on essential needs, consult a realtor, and schedule a home inspection.
- Financial strategies: Consider additional income sources and prepare for unforeseen expenses.
- Mortgage approach: Seek a mortgage reflecting your financial standing; ensure all documents are in order.

**Post-approval preparedness:**

- Ensure your credit remains is in good condition by paying all your obligations on time.
- Avoid major purchases that could affect your financial stability.
- Set aside funds for unexpected costs.
- Have your lawyer review you're your purchase agreement and closing documents.

## DECLARING WAR ON YOUR MORTGAGE

GP: "Paying off a mortgage swiftly should be a priority, especially when interest rates are high. Paying extra on the principle early on will significantly cut down both the mortgage term and the total interest paid.

Charles: Correct declare war on your mortgage but not on your emergency savings it needs to balance. Here are key mortgage reduction tactics:

- Incrementally increase mortgage payments.
- Apply tax refunds from you RRSP contribution against your mortgage balance.
- Opt for accelerated bi-weekly payments.
- Take advantage of double-up options.
- Round up your payments to the nearest hundred.
- Submit lump sum payments when possible.
- Maintain current payments if you negotiate a lower interest rate.
- Always balance this with maintaining emergency funds and investments."

Charles: "It's a balancing act! We aim to make extra payments without sacrificing our investment growth in TFSAs and RRSPs."

GP: "Exactly! Paying down a mortgage faster means less waste and more savings, like fine-tuning an engine, but never at the cost of reducing emergency or long-term savings."

Charles: "GP, you once tackled a $196,000 mortgage. What was your strategy?"

GP: "We cut back sharply. Swapped a new car for an older one, put the savings to the mortgage, and spared a bit for investments. We treated ourselves modestly while enjoying some fun activities which kept morale high without breaking the bank."

Charles: "And the result?"

GP: "Victory in six years instead of twelve. Not only did we become mortgage-free, but we also learned lasting financial habits and safeguarded our future funds."

Charles: "Incredible! A true lesson in discipline and focus."

## BECOMING A SAVVY ESTATE INVESTOR

"Landlords grow wealthy in their sleep..."

—John Stuart Mill

GP: "The secret behind many wealthy investors is simple: they start with just one property, and with financial rewards, they dive deeper."

Charles: "Every mansion starts with a single brick; it's all about taking that initial step."

GP: "Indeed. Buying a first property is like learning to ride a bike with training wheels—it prepares you for bigger challenges. To start, make sure your emergency fund is solid. Then, gather your financial crew: your mortgage agent, advisor, and lender. Use your assets wisely but protect your emergency fund. Work with your real estate agent to find properties with good rental potential. Ask a thorough cost analysis and plan for future expenses, focusing on multi-unit properties with reliable income, like those with basement rentals. If there's someone reliable, think about teaming up—two minds are better than one in property deals. This approach will smooth out the process of getting pre-approvals for future buys."

Charles: "I see market ups and downs as challenges, not roadblocks. With careful asset management, strategic partnerships, and thorough research, I aim to capitalize on market opportunities. Now that I am settled in my home, I plan to borrow on the equity that is built to buy my first investment property. The goal? To develop a steady stream of passive income to support my retirement comfortably."

## WHO IS YOUR SUPPORT SYSTEM?

GP: "If you want to really get ahead in real estate, you need a Cadillac support system. I know Cathie always asked me who was mine when I wanted to buy a new property.

"Here's a list of the different professionals needed:

- Real estate lawyers must act on your behalf through purchases, refinances, property searches, and even condo issues.
- Real estate agents can assemble the most advantageous purchase and sale agreements with professionalism, patience, and integrity. They also identify red flags and accuracies.
- Mortgage brokers should be good teachers, making good suggestions, addressing your budget, and focusing not just on what they can offer you today but ensuring you can still afford it tomorrow.
- Paralegals and property managers can assist with landlord-tenant issues for real estate investors. They help to make sure you fulfill your important duties and obligations.
- Tax experts are vital to ensure you're filing all the necessary declarations for principal residences and investment property tax strategies.
- Handymen and contractors should be carefully vetted. Get references and do your homework to find those you can count on.
- Financial planners can give advice on budgeting and saving for your down payment, keeping your next steps on solid ground.
- Like-minded investors can share their experiences and help you avoid real estate pitfalls. Remember, you become who you surround yourself with!"

Charles: "The motto here is, 'When in doubt, seek help!' No one gets very far down the road of life without a great support system. I don't know how it was back when you first started buying property, but clients tell me it feels nearly impossible to get qualified these days. With the cost of homes, it makes it worse! Here are a few tips that can help when the thought of buying a home seems like going up a mountain in winter with your summer tires on."

GP: "I suggest meeting with a mortgage agent to plan your mortgage financing, as they have access to all types of lenders, meaning it will be more gear towards your needs You'll know the income and down payment you need. Yes, you may need to consider a second job, but trust me, it will be worth it!"

Charles: "Develop a two or three-year plan with your mortgage agent and financial advisor, one that gives you time but not so far away that you lose focus on your goal."

GP: "Look at down payment strategies such as RRSP or FHSA tax refunds, gifts from immediate relatives, equity from other properties, and revenue from a second job or overtime hours. Sometimes lines of credit can be used if it makes sense."

Charles: "Talk to immediate family members who may be able to co-sign and remove their names in a year or two."

GP: "Check out properties with possible revenues. Two friends might consider buying a duplex, where each has their own apartment. Both incomes can be used to qualify."

> **NUTS AND BOLTS**

- Home buying: an excellent investment that necessitates meticulous planning and strategic thinking.

- Professional consultation: always engage with mortgage experts and financial advisors before starting the journey. Pre-approval is a must.

- Balance in payments: align mortgage payments with your overall budget, considering crucial savings like TFSAs and RRSPs. It's about financial equilibrium.

- First-home considerations: your initial home doesn't need to be a dream one. Upgrade as your wealth expands; evolve with your financial growth.

- Mortgage-free versus portfolio growth: analyze if being mortgage-free aligns with your goals or if you aim to expand your investment portfolio. Tailor your approach.

- Strong support system: cultivate a robust support network, including professionals and like-minded investors. It's a team effort.

- Market fluctuations: treat changes in the housing market as opportunities, not setbacks. Adapt to thrive, verify possible benefits of careful technics to grow your real estate portfolio.

**NOTE:** The savings plan types discussed in this chapter are specific to Canada, although the guidelines and steps for the real estate journey may be similar in other countries.

# A LITTLE INSPIRATION

## A Deer in the Forest

Once, a doe with chestnut fur lived in a lush forest by the sea. She enjoyed the peaceful life among the trees and the gentle lapping of the waves. However, a twist of fate caused her to lose vision in one eye. To protect herself, she always kept her sight toward the forest, trusting that the sea was a friend, not a foe.

The doe's caution was like a shield, her own form of insurance against the perils of the woods. Yet, the sea, with its vast mysteries, held dangers she hadn't anticipated. One fateful day, while grazing in her beloved meadow, a band of fishermen approached from the waters, a direction she had considered safe.

The doe was caught off guard, her attention fixed on the forest. The fishermen, driven by hunger, saw an opportunity and took it. The doe, once a vigilant guardian of her well-being, became a meal for weary travelers.

This tale is a somber reminder that danger can come from unexpected places, and preparation for one threat might leave us vulnerable to others. It speaks to the importance of comprehensive protection, much like insurance in our lives. It safeguards us against the risks we anticipate and those we cannot predict. Life is unpredictable just like the forest and the sea, and our vigilance must be cast in all directions.

CHAPTER 14

# PROTECTION FROM THE STORM

*"We cannot prevent the unexpected."*
—AESOP

As we continue our financial journey, we now find ourselves at a juncture where we need to think about sheltering from potential storms. After all, the road to financial stability can be a challenging ride. Just like a sturdy umbrella protects you from rain, insurance protects your loved ones and assets from life's unpredictable storms. This chapter will arm you with an understanding of various insurance types, helping you ensure that your hard-earned wealth is not only well-managed but also well-protected.

**ASK YOURSELF:**

- Do I have enough of the right insurance coverage (health, life, property, etc.)?
- Have I considered potential financial risks and how to mitigate them?

After years of navigating the finance world as a planner, Charles found himself eager to discuss a crucial aspect of wealth management: protecting assets and loved ones. Despite his degree in finance, he always took advantage of every opportunity to soak up GP's advice, sometime valuing these garage chats more than his university lecture hall. The combination of GP's wisdom and Charles's technical knowledge perfectly blended old and new perspectives. Together, they ventured into the often-overlooked realm of insurance, ready to tackle the complexities head-on.

## WHO DO YOU NEED TO PROTECT?

Charles: "Remember how we turned a toy car into an impenetrable tank using duct tape. I think of insurance as that essential duct tape—it shields us from the unexpected crashes in life. Imagine the heartbreak if our beloved vintage car was uninsured and got scratched. That's the kind of tragedy our loved one's face when we leave them unprotected."

GP: "Absolutely, you're right! Your cousin Sam's sudden passing, just before his twenty-third birthday, reminds us of life's unpredictability. The financial strain on his grieving family could have been avoided had he been insured. Tragically, he met with Cathie the week before the accident, who had suggested a solid insurance plan. Sam, still young, chose to think it over. His family ended up taking a loan to cover his funeral expenses."

Charles: "A mere $50 a month for insurance could have secured his wife and future child with a means to replace his income and sustain their home."

GP: "I view insurance as our financial airbag. It softens the blow of any financial crash that might affect our family."

Charles: "It's tough convincing my young clients, who often feel invincible and prefer spending on entertainment over what they see as 'boring' insurance."

GP: "Share your cousin tragic story. Youth doesn't exempt us from life's mishaps. Plus, insurance is more affordable when you're young and healthy. Why gamble with your family's financial future by speeding through life without the safety of insurance?"

Charles: "Just as we wouldn't drive a car without auto insurance, we shouldn't navigate life without life insurance to protect our loved ones."

## TYPES OF INSURANCE: YOUR PROTECTION TOOLBOX

Charles: "Insurance isn't one-size-fits-all. It's like a mechanic's toolbox, different tools for different needs."

### At a Glance: Protecting the Ones You Love

**Life Insurance:** This is crucial for securing your loved ones' financial future. It provides a death benefit to your beneficiaries, ensuring they have financial support after you're gone.

**Term Insurance:** Cost-effective and temporary, this insurance is like renting what you need without the high cost of buying. It's perfect for covering specific debts, like a mortgage, during the time you need it most.

**Whole Life Insurance:** Unlike term insurance, whole life insurance covers you for your entire life. You can choose from basic plans to more comprehensive ones with added features like cash values or the potential to earn dividends. This type of insurance supports you later in life and benefits your loved ones.

**Disability Insurance:** If you can't work due to an injury or illness, this insurance acts as your financial backup, replacing your income during tough times.

**Critical Illness Insurance:** Think of this as your safety net if you face a serious illness. It provides a lump sum to cover your expenses and medical bills, allowing you to focus solely on recovery. Some policies may even refund your premiums if no claims are made, like a no-claim bonus with car insurance.

**Group Employee Insurance:** Offered by employers, this is similar to term insurance but tied to your job. It ends when your employment does unless you convert it into a personal policy beforehand.

**Mortgage Insurance:** This coverag specifically pays off your mortgage in case something happens to you. It's useful but before buying consider whether if your family might also need cash for other expenses.

**Home Insurance:** This coverage protects your home from theft, fire, or flood. Make sure your coverage limits and deductibles fit your budget.

**Car Insurance:** Essential for peace of mind on the road, this insurance covers you in case of accidents, lawsuits, or theft.

Charles: "To determine the right amount of insurance, we must consider when the coverage is needed, how it aligns with our specific needs and our financial goals."

GP: "We must ensure that every aspect of our life is well-protected, just like having a well-equipped toolbox for any mechanical job."

Charles: "Cathie was instrumental in my education about insurance. She emphasized the importance of asking specific questions to identify a client's needs accurately:

- What is your current net worth, including all assets and subtracting liabilities?
- Who do you intend to protect with your insurance coverage?
- How much annual income is required to ensure your loved ones maintain their standard of living without financial hardship?
- How long will your family need the income support provided by the insurance?
- What will be your final expenses, and what potential tax liabilities could be incurred at your death?

First, we figure out the right coverage amount. Then, we delve deeper into deciding if it will be permanent or term insurance much like buying a well equipped car.

GP: "I have never heard a widow say she received too much life insurance. Sadly, it is usually the opposite."

> **LET'S PLAY: PERMANENT VS TERM INSURANCE**
>
> Imagine this scenario where Sylvie and Peter, both 25 years old, are deciding on a $250,000 insurance policy.
>
> **Sylvie** opts for a whole life policy, costing her $135 per month. She prefers the security of maintaining her coverage for life. It's a bit like buying a car—more costly upfront, but it's yours to keep forever.
>
> **Peter**, on the other hand, goes for term insurance, which costs him just $25 per month. This is like leasing a car: more affordable initially, but once the lease is up, continuing coverage can get pricey.
>
> Fast forward 40 years to age 65. Sylvie still enjoys the benefits of her insurance, while Peter's term insurance has expired, and renewing it at his current age is prohibitively expensive. If Peter had been diligent in investing the difference between his term insurance and Sylvie's whole life premium, he could have amassed an investment worth $265,000. Unfortunately, he didn't save the difference, leaving him unprotected, whereas Sylvie continues to have her insurance safeguarding her loved ones.
>
> In this game of life, Sylvie emerges as the winner, making a well-informed decision based on her needs. Peter, who initially chose what seemed a cost-effective option, ended up short-handed due to lack of planning. Buying insurance, much like buying a car, requires thorough research and a careful assessment of your budget.

GP: "The moral of the story is... always consult a licensed insurance professional to choose the right type of insurance."

Charles: "Correct GP, much like deciding whether to rent or own a home. Always be upfront about any health conditions and ensure you fully understand the terms of your insurance policy."

GP: "Correct! Never forget, the most valuable asset to insure is yourself!"

Charles: "By staying focused on managing our finances, we trust that our insurance will smooth out rough patches."

GP: "Let's secure that safety net and drive confidently into the future. Insurance it is, don't leave home without it."

> **NUTS AND BOLTS**
>
> - Insurance is protection from the storm.
> - Dust off and review your insurance policies.
> - Make an appointment with your financial advisor.
> - Protect your most valuable asset—yourself!
> - Good planning brings peace of mind!
> - This is your family's future, and it is in your hands.
>
> Make it RIGHT for those you **LOVE!**

"A penny saved is a penny earned."
—Benjamin Franklin

## A LITTLE INSPIRATION
### The Origins of the Piggy Bank

Back then, people didn't have online banking or stylish wallets. They used pots made from affordable clay called "pygg" to stash their extra coins. It wasn't as sexy as a Gucci wallet, but it worked!

One day, a cheery potter, let's call him Jerr, noted that "pygg" sounded a lot like "pig." Now, Jerr had a peculiar sense of humor. He also noticed that real-life pigs loved to roll in the pygg mud. So, after a jolly evening of medieval mead, Bob thought, What a hoot! I'll shape this boring pygg pot into a pig!

Word spread faster than a castle gossip, and before Jerr knew it, his workshop was swarmed with folks demanding these hilarious pig-shaped pygg pots. Potters everywhere were cranking out these piggy pots like hotcakes, each cuter than the last!

Over time, "pygg" became less about clay and more about the oink. And that's how the piggy bank, our beloved financial sidekick, was born. The result of a linguistic mix-up, a muddy pig, and a potter's joke that went "viral." So, folks, remember, every time you drop a coin into a piggy bank, you're chuckling along with a joke that's been running for centuries! Now, that's a legacy!

CHAPTER 15

# GET THE KIDS INVOLVED

*"This piggy bank is for your hopes and schemes.
To help you save for all your dreams."*
—GP

Money isn't an inherited trait but a learned skill. As parents, we often worry about leaving our children drive our hefty car equipped with all the bells and whistles; however, isn't it more important to ensure they know how to drive it? Our true wealth lies not in the material possessions we give but, in the knowledge, and values we instill. As we navigate the financial freeway, remember to take our children along for the ride. Let's roll our sleeves, pop the hood, and involve the kids in this financial road trip!

**ASK YOURSELF:**

- Am I setting a good example for my children?
- Do I take time to play Money games with my kids?
- Do we involve our children in financial decisions?
- How are my kids doing with their Money, now?

GP watched with a tender smile as Charles guided little Eric into the garage. Eric's eyes lit up when he saw a colorful ceramic piggy bank waiting on the workbench, GP's heartfelt present for his great-grandson. It was a symbol of hope for a future of financial security, inscribed with an encouraging message: "Save here for your hopes and dreams." In Eric's eager grasp of the piggy bank, GP saw the same promise as a young person holding their first car keys—a world of potential opening. As GP's eyes sparkled with joy, he envisioned the day Eric would realize the worth of this early investment in his dreams.

GP: "Ah, a young mind ready for financial adventures! It's important to start early, as the lessons you learn in finance will stay with you forever!"

GP: "Who's this, Eric?" Leaning down, GP pointed to the piggy bank.

Charles: "That's Penny the Piggy Bank, Eric. It will teach you that saving now is the fast track to your future dreams."

## TEACHING YOUR KIDS ABOUT MONEY

GP bent down to Eric and drew from his pocket a playful little green pouch that Grandma had crafted. It resembled a cheerful alien with bright eyes and a shiny nose that seemed to welcome its new owner. Handing it over to Eric, GP's warm smile broadened.

GP: "Here you go, this is MONEY, your new friend who will help you learn and have fun saving!"

Charles: "How about we start filling it with some coins?"

## RESPONSIBILITY TO OUR CHILDREN

GP: "Just as I once passed on my knowledge about car fixing and Money handling to you, now it's your time to teach these valuable lessons to Eric. It's time to continue our family tradition. Teach Eric as I taught you. Guide him to 'pay himself first' with the help of his new friend, MONEY. This way, he'll learn early to save some of what he gets, avoiding debt and running toward financial independence."

Charles: "Absolutely, GP. Our open conversations about Money have set the foundation for my financial planning career. Now, I'll pass on that wisdom to Eric, who will start feeding MONEY pouch his coins."

GP: "Indeed. I would like to add one more thing: teach Eric the joy of earning his own Money. He will feel a sense of achievement when he earns from doing chores. And let's not forget about the joy of giving. Encourage him to donate a small part of his earnings or savings to a cause he cares about. It will give him a sense of satisfaction that Money just can't buy!"

## LEAD BY EXAMPLE

GP: "It makes me proud that you're teaching Eric about Money. You're setting him up with the right tools early in life so that he won't get stuck on the wrong side of the road of finance."

Charles: "Absolutely! We're trying to shape his habits now so that he doesn't think ATMs are just magical vending machines."

GP: "Think of it like teaching him to navigate with a map before giving him the car keys. Before heading out on the highway, he needs to first drive around the block."

Charles: "Jessie's already repurposed my first dream board for him to use. We know that one day, he'll need to steer his financial path. We're leading by example now, so he'll be ready when it's his turn. It's like a game of Simon Says with Money."

## MAKE IT EASY AND FUN

GP: "Think of it as turning financial education into a fun road trip instead of an unpleasant traffic jam. A few games here, some interesting apps there, and before you know it, learning about Money is as exciting."

Charles: "Absolutely. I've saved our family's game board, that has brought us so many entertaining Sundays. It would be quite the sight, to play Monopoly with real money. I can imagine Eric wanting to buy every space he lands on! But let's save my wallet from that adventure; we'll keep playing with Monopoly Money and use finance apps for his learning."

GP: "Here is a great way to teach Eric a savings game. Hide coins at home as a treasure hunt, where finding each coin teaches Money lessons. Nickels encourage saving for small treats, dimes are for earning through chores, and quarters help learn about buying essentials. A loonie represents saving for future wants, and a toonie suggests taking on more tasks for more Money.

After playing, Eric will put 20% of his coins in his piggy bank and the remainder in his Money pouch, teaching him about saving and the value of Money. It's a fun way to grow his savings and learn financial basics."

GP: "It's impressive how he planned his budget with Money. Doing small jobs to earn and being frugal. Also, I see he fed Piggy his 10% for the long term. What a great job, kiddo!"

Charles: "Indeed! Out of the $185.00 from his birthday present, he put $18.50 (10%) into Piggy and the remaining $166.50 in his green pouch. He's been wisely allocating his earnings every time. The first 10% goes into Piggy, the portion for wants into his wallet (colored pencils and chocolate), and the remaining balance goes into MONEY, the guardian of his dream, the first one being a telescope."

GP: "And I saw his mini budget sheet Well, done. Not to mention the notebook, full of stars representing his savings for that dream!"

Charles: "Eric bought the telescope after just one year of saving for it!"

GP: "And tonight, as he gazes through it, the stars will shine just for him. Now let's talk about tackling Money when he is in high school!"

## FINANCES 101 IN HIGH SCHOOL

Charles: "As I see it, high school is when we need to put the pedal to the metal to build financial literacy. We need to switch lanes from basic Money matters to teaching about debit cards, bills, debt, budgeting, and savings. By the end of this ride, Eric should feel comfortable taking the wheel for his financial journey with MONEY as his co-pilot."

GP: "High school isn't just about Shakespeare and trigonometry; it's also about learning to avoid the stress of credit card debt and appreciate the magic of compound interest. And if we teach him right, Eric will be a financial whizz who won't mistake Dad's Bank for a drive-thru every time he's running low on cash!"

Charles: "I attribute a great part of my financial expertise to you. School equipped me with the mechanics to be a financial advisor, but your wisdom fine-tuned me to become a financially savvy individual. You and Grandma taught me to be frugal. Grandparents have a wealth of knowledge and can play a crucial role in fueling their grandchildren's understanding of Money. I am a testament to that."

GP: "Teaching you, my children, and grandchildren about Money has been one of the greatest joy rides of my life!"

Charles: "Inspired by your teachings, I've drafted a 'GP's Money Legacy checklist. It's sort of a roadmap for financial understanding and growth. What do you think?

## GP'S LEGACY OF FINANCIAL WISDOM

- "Our Sunday dinners were lessons in family history and Money management where we'd discuss our ancestors' homes, cars, and their savings journey, often poring over old family photos.
- GP and Grandma enriched our lives with cultural outings, teaching us to handle Money by counting out cash for treats like ice cream.
- Games were educational, too; GP used to place a loonie on the cribbage table, with the winner contributing to their Money pouch or Piggy.
- Our dream boards were a source of pride, especially during Sunday dinners, where stories earned us a loonie, encouraging our narrative skills.
- GP's collection of foreign coins from travels turned into a guessing game, rewarding correct guesses with the coin, sparking Eric's interest in this game.
- I graduated debt-free due to GP's foresight in opening bank accounts for us and giving monetary gifts for birthdays and special events, coupled with my parents' RESP contributions.

Charles: GP, you've been a guiding force in shaping our attitudes about Money. You showed us how to flip negative notions into positive actions. Do you remember the time I told you my friend Joey said Money was evil? You answered it's not Money but its intention, teaching us to value honest work and the Money we earn."

## NUTS AND BOLTS

Financial literacy is essential; teach it to your children.

- It is never too early to learn Money skills.
- Make it FUN and challenging.
- Teach your child the benefit of saving.
- Examine your attitudes and Money beliefs.
- Let them handle Money and accept they could make different choices.
- Model good Money strategies.
- Show children the importance of putting their dreams into action.
- Be honest with your children.
- Teach them to be frugal, not cheap.

Get your child a piggy bank and craft them a MONEY pouch

# A LITTLE INSPIRATION

## Lesson from the Wise Old Mane

In a Himalayan village, an elderly sage was revered for his wisdom. A young boy, aiming to challenge him, concealed a bird in his hands and asked the senior if it was alive or dead. He thought he could counteract any answer that the sage would give. With years of life's lessons behind him, the sage smiled and said, "The bird's fate is in your hands." The elder's point was clear: life's outcomes depend on our choices.

## FROM GP'S JOKE BOX

On his deathbed, a wealthy, stingy old man begs his long-suffering wife to bury his fortune with him. She solemnly agrees. At the funeral, just before the coffin is sealed, she tucks a small metal box beside him. Terrified, her friend whispers, "You didn't really put the Money in there, did you?" The widow nods, "I kept my promise. I gathered all his Money, deposited it in my account, and wrote him a check."

**CHAPTER 16**

# TAKING CARE OF SENIORS

*"Money is like a sixth sense, and you can't make use of the other five without it."*
—WILLIAM SOMERSET MAUGHAM

Entering retirement should be a serene and secure time, fostered by smart saving and wise investing. It's a period for reflection and enjoyment yet preparing for changing financial needs is crucial. It involves safeguarding seniors' independence and offering support to ensure a dignified and fulfilling life.

When considering how best to assist seniors with financial matters, it's crucial to **ask yourself:**

- Do I possess the know-how to guide seniors through managing their finances effectively?
- Am I vigilant about protecting seniors from financial scams that disproportionately target them?

- Have I ensured that the seniors in my care have a comprehensive and up-to-date estate plan to secure their legacy?

Even though Charles wasn't close to his retirement, he was eager to absorb GP's advice to better guide his elderly clients through their financial landscapes.

## RETIREMENT AND THE SENIOR MILESTONE

GP: "Becoming a senior is like crossing the finish line. It's not just about the age count; it's about changing gears and entering a new phase of life with new attitudes and social benefits."

Charles: "It comes with perks—discounts, travel deals, and more that allow you to enjoy the ride in life's luxury lane."

GP: "To ensure that seniors can enjoy a comfortable and fulfilling retirement, numerous benefits are offered, such as:

- Retail discounts
- Tax deductions
- Social security payments
- Affordable health insurance
- Specialized senior services.

These perks make essential and luxury items more afford-able, supporting seniors in their golden years."

Charles: "Retirement means a transition from fast-paced work to a richer, more leisure-centered stage of life. It's akin to shifting from racing to enjoying a scenic road trip, valuing the views over velocity."

GP: "That's right. It's natural to feel a bit anxious before embarking on this new adventure. The key is having a good look at our financial plans to ensure a smooth ride into retirement."

Charles: "With life expectancies rising, a solid financial plan fuels this extended journey, making it worry-free."

GP: "Precisely. When advising seniors, explain to them that it is better to have a consistent income instead of continuing to accumulate savings. It is also important that they understand tax impacts and the benefits of phased withdrawals."

Charles: "I understand. It's about guiding them through gradual income strategies and the perks of tax-free accounts like TFSAs for flexibility."

GP: "Good. And don't forget to explain the retirement benefits in Canada—CPP and QPP. These are designed to supplement their income post-retirement."

Charles: "I'll be sure to personalize the advice, considering their own circumstances, health, and whether they're single or have a partner."

GP: "Exactly, remember, it's essential to explore all assets they might leverage, like property or reverse mortgages, to bolster their income."

This discussion highlights the importance of holistic planning in retirement. Charles appreciates that advising seniors means understanding their changing needs. A flexible retirement plan provides them with peace of mind, regardless of what may come. After all, these are their golden years!

## NAVIGATING POST-RETIREMENT WORK AND BENEFITS

GP: "Navigate your senior clients so they see their savings like a fuel tank and guide them on how to use that fuel efficiently."

Charles: "Retirement does not always mean a full stop; many people pause before returning to work part-time or even full-time."

GP: "True. Many seniors go back to work for extra cash or to stay active. But working in retirement has its twists and turns."

Charles: "Absolutely. Earning too much could chip away at your Old Age Security pension, reducing it incrementally based on your income."

GP: "Don't forget, you and your employer must contribute to CPP until you are 65, which can boost your benefits later."

Charles: "Indeed. Waiting to collect OAS or CPP/QPP until 70 can supercharge your benefits. Once you start collecting, though, the amount is set, except for possible spousal transfers. By delaying benefits until 70, we ensure a longer, more comfortable ride. But remember, our benefits end with us unless we have a spouse to pass them on to. Retirement planning is complex. Hence, navigating it with a financial advisor is best."

GP: "Exactly, it is complex. It's like driving a sports car—accelerate too fast by cashing out RRSPs early, and you could overshoot benefit thresholds. It's all about cruising at the right pace."

**FRAUD PREVENTION**

GP: "Seniors' financial protection is a priority. Just as we protect classic cars from damage, we must guard our elderly against scams that lurk online or over the phone. It's essential to stay vigilant and get a second opinion if something feels off."

Charles: "It's heartbreaking seeing scammers target seniors. It's just wrong. Seniors need a clear, trusted guide to avoid financial scams, just like a car needs a good alarm system. We must help them protect their finances with care and the right safeguards."

GP: "Just as we'd store a vintage car in a secure garage, we need to give seniors the tools to safely manage and protect their Money. Whether it's safe banking habits or reliable advice, it's about ensuring their financial vehicle stays in prime condition."

Charles: "What's the best way to prevent such incidents?"

GP: "The first step is awareness. As you'd verify a mechanic's credentials, seniors must be cautious of unsolicited calls and emails. When in doubt, it's best to consult someone they trust. It's always better to have a second pair of eyes or ears in car terms, a co-driver to help navigate potential threats."

Charles: "Some seniors face financial abuse from their own families. How can we safeguard against this?"

GP: "Unfortunately, it's a grim reality. The key is education and conversation. Just as a car owner might invest in a security system, seniors should have regular conversations with trusted financial advisors or legal counsel. Understanding tools like power of attorney and having clear documentation can be as vital as a car's anti-theft system. It's all about setting up defenses and being aware."

Charles: "The other day, a lovely lady named Justine, 65 years young, walk into my office in tears. You know those classic cars that need a paint job, but everything is still pristine under the hood? Justine bought a house like that. Three units, run-down, but structurally sound."

GP: "I can see where this is going. Please tell me she had a builder, or a home inspector check it out first?"

Charles: "She did, but that's where the problem started. Justine had a cousin, Tom, who was a general contractor. She trusted him, and he seemed to have her best interest at heart. He said, 'I know some guys, they aren't working right now. You pay them their hourly wage plus the materials, and we'll get the job done.' Seemed like a win-win."

GP: "It was not a win-win situation."

Charles: "No! It was more like buying a shiny new car but getting stuck with a clunker. The guys started ripping the place apart. They replaced things that didn't need replacing and skipped things that did.

It was a jumble of repairs. Plumbing, electricity, heating—you name it. They left Justine with an astronomical bill of over 600K!"

GP: "Oh no, that sounds like she's been taken for a ride!"

Charles: "Exactly! Instead of coasting smoothly into retirement, she ended up with a financial fender-bender. And all of this could have been avoided with more caution and a solid contract. Justine knows 'who took her money' all too well."

GP: "Sadly, it's a common situation. Many seniors, trusting and kind-hearted, often fall prey to such scenarios, assuming others are as genuine as they are."

## CASH MANAGEMENT

GP: "Let's keep sight of the basics, like oil changes and tire rotations or, in financial terms, cash management. Maintaining a healthy financial flow is as crucial as keeping a car's oil clean, especially for those near the retirement pit stop."

Charles: "You're right. We are responsible for protecting our seniors' financial health just as we give our beloved old cars the TLC they need. They've steered us through life's highways and byways; it's only fair we help ensure their financial journey remains smooth and worry-free."

## THE TRUE WEALTH OF SENIOR WELL-BEING

Charles: "After consulting advisors and dodging scam attempts, I've come to realize something about our senior years: it's not solely about finances. True wealth during this phase encompasses the well-being of our mind, body, and social connections."

## NUTS AND BOLTS

- Meet an advisor to discuss changes to your plan, income sources, and government benefits.
- Get tax advice on how working post-retirement will benefit you and affect your income through relevant strategies.
- Be cautious about texts, emails, and calls asking for personal, credit card, or banking information.
- Check out local seniors' groups and services through local community associations.
- Keep active while investing in your mental, physical, and financial health.

# A LITTLE INSPIRATION

## Together Everyone Accomplishes Miracles

I wish my arms could reach across the miles, giving you a big hug!

One night, I woke up, sat at my desk, and drew a picture of a little bear giving a hug. (This was bizarre because I can't draw!) My daughter's best friend was losing her battle with cancer. This triggered the memory of the wonderful friends that I had also lost to cancer, and my little inner voice urged me to do something. It all began with the belief of Patrick McNulty, Counselor, and André Potvin, Principal of St. Matthew High School in Orléans, ON.

That's when family, friends, students, and community members rallied to heighten public awareness and raise funds for cancer research and patient care by participating in a huge "bear hug" around the Ottawa Rideau Canal.

The miracle of giving had taken place. Students and counselors at St. Matthew High School took on the Bear Hug Challenge. The event was a great success, breaking the Guinness World record and generating $108,000 to donate to cancer research and patient care.

Four years later, the TEAM created a second bear hug that spanned both sides of the Rideau Canal, from Laurier Street to the Pretoria Bridge. That day, many of us smiled through tears as we hugged, remembering the friends and loved ones we had lost. Thanks to the spirit and dedication of the 11,000 students committed to finding a cure for cancer, we raised three times more Money than the first bear hug!

Born from my desire to give back, the Bear Hug Project succeeded in uniting a whole community while providing hope, love, and inspiration.

Monique Gagné (*formely Amyot*) is the founder of the largest bear hug.

CHAPTER 17

# LEAVING A LEGACY

*"You have not lived a perfect day, even though you have earned your Money, unless you have done something for someone who will never be able to repay you."*
—RUTH SMELTZER

In today's world, instant gratification often overshadows the lasting benefits of saving Money. It's important to remember that leaving a legacy is more than just financial wealth; it includes the wisdom we pass down to future generations. As we navigate the challenge of saving in an age of immediate rewards, we look at ways to combine classic saving strategies with modern technology. Our goal is to create an impact beyond our lifetime, ensuring our legacy is rich in guidance and financial support for the paths we've set for others.

**ASK YOURSELF:**

- Have I sufficiently planned for my loved ones' financial well-being after my passing?
- Is my will current, and does my estate plan reflect my last wishes?

- What do I want my legacy to be?

Charles entered GP's garage, where reminders of the past fueled contemplations of the future. Here, memories and aspirations converged, much like the vintage car that stands as a symbol of legacy.

## THE GIFT OF RESPONSIBILITY

GP: "No one has ever become poor by giving. True happiness lies in generosity, which echoes through time. What legacy do you intend to create?"

Charles: "Mom and Cathie say that Money is the currency of love. The joy we got from donating our restored classic car was priceless."

GP: "Indeed. Money is a tool whose value is enriched by intention. It's not the amount that we accumulate, but the difference we make with it."

Charles: "I always include 'giving' in my financial choices."

GP: "Well learned, son! True wealth comes from the ability to give. Have you felt the joy of giving a gift or the satisfaction of contributing to a cause? Generosity enriches us."

Charles: "Absolutely. It's about giving time, energy, and understanding, not just Money. That's where true wealth is found."

## GIVING BACK TO CHARITY

Charles: "We build our finances and care for our loved ones. Then comes a time to enjoy the rewards of our hard work. At the same time, we can support our favorite charities in ways that benefit both the causes we admire and our tax situation. Some methods include:

- Annual cash gifts that bring yearly tax receipts.
- Leaving assets or property in your will can bring joy to a charity and give you a tax receipt.

- Donating stocks as a legacy. These are free from capital gains tax, and the more you give, the more you save on taxes.
- Using life insurance as a donation tool is powerful. With just the monthly premium, you can leave a significant gift after you pass. Set up correctly, you can deduct the premiums annually or get a big tax credit to reduce the taxes after you're gone. This way, life insurance can leave a significant legacy."

GP: "Just like a well-maintained car runs smoothly, a well-planned financial life cares for us and helps others. It's the oil that keeps the engine of life running well."

Charles: "Cathie and I talked about our legacy goals, and on her advice, I bought extra life insurance with the Money I usually give to charity. Can you believe it? I got a $500,000 policy. I get a tax receipt each year, and when I'm gone, my favorite charity gets $500,000. It's a gift I never thought I could give."

## WHERE DOES MY MONEY GO WHEN I DIE?

GP: "Where your Money ends up after you die depends largely on whether you have a will, and if it's up-to-date. If not, your assets might unintentionally go to an outdated beneficiary, or even to the government if you have no remaining family members."

Charles: "It's very important to have a will to direct our last wishes. The only truly valid will is a formal one made by a lawyer or a notary. If that's impossible, a handwritten one is still better than none. Make sure it is handwritten and witnessed."

GP: "We should all review our will every five years or after major life events like marriage or divorce. Remember, a divorce doesn't automatically cancel your will. Always keep a copy of the will for yourself and give one to your executor."

Charles: "Also, consider a power of attorney for your property. This way, you will have someone you trust manage your affairs if you can't. Lawyers often prepare a will and a power of attorney simultaneously."

GP: "Imagine if you had separated and were raising your children on your own but forgot to update your will after separation and you passed away. You could be leaving all your Money to your ex, who would still be the primary beneficiary in your will or perhaps even a life insurance policy!"

Charles: "Often, a legal separation doesn't affect a will. A divorce doesn't generally revoke a will either, but in many jurisdictions, a divorce will revoke certain provisions in a will. That's why it's important to get advice from a professional. Now that I have a family, I want to make sure all my assets go to them after my passing."

GP: "You inspire me, son, as you understand the importance of a will. I wish everyone would take the time to tend to this responsibility."

Charles: "Taxes are owed by the deceased's estate, reducing what's left if you leave a specific asset to a child or grandchild. Naming a grandchild as the beneficiary on a tax-free savings account, an RRSP, a RRIF, or a similar account means it passes outside your estate and goes directly to the grandchild like an insurance policy."

GP: "That's right. A good mechanic understands every detail of a car, and similarly, understanding the intricacies of financial tools is key.

Charles: "Exactly! It's not just about transferring assets but also minimizing 'repair costs'—taxes—so the full value of the inheritance is received. Tools like tax-free savings accounts or registered retirement plans can streamline this."

GP: "Like maintaining our classic cars, we must plan our finances for a smooth transition to our loved ones as well.

**Here are a few assets that are covered by the will:**

- Assets registered in your sole name.
- Assets registered as tenancy in common; for example, a cottage owned by two families.
- Shares or debt obligations of publicly traded corporations.
- Any assets in the estate's name (such as a life insurance policy or RRSPs that name the estate as the beneficiary).

**Assets that do not flow through the will:**

- Assets that have a named beneficiary, such as life insurance, an RRSP, RRIF, or RPP.
- Assets owned as joint tenants with right of survivorship.
- Shares or debt obligations of a private corporation.
- Assets covered by a pre-nuptial agreement or cohabitation agreement.
- Business interests that are part of a buy-sell agreement.
- Assets in a living trust."

## DYING WITHOUT A WILL (INTESTATE)

Charles: "If you die intestate, your possessions are distributed according to the laws where you live. Dying without a will is like a car running wild without a driver."

GP: "And if you have a common-law spouse, they might not be recognized as you'd wish. What about the children who depend on you?"

Charles: "The court will decide on their guardian, and the children will only receive their inheritance when they come of age."

GP: "The spouse doesn't automatically get everything. Some of the estate could be allocated to the children. Are there delays in settling the estate if there's no will?"

Charles: "Absolutely! Without a clear will, the estate could face higher taxes. The deceased's final wishes might be overlooked, and if no relatives are found, the estate could eventually go to the government."

---

**HOW TO WRITE A WILL**

(This Will must be handwritten)

THIS IS MY LAST WILL AND TESTAMENT.

I, the undersigned, [last name, first name, social insurance number] being of sound mind and memory, declare this to be my last WILL and TESTAMENT.

I revoke all prior Wills and Testaments at any time heretofore made by me. I give and bequeath [determine beneficiaries and property].

I appoint_____as Executor of my Will.

I give instructions to pay all just debts, funeral, and testamentary expenses.

Signed and dated at [City and Province] on this_____day of_____, 20_____

Your signature

---

Charles: "Depending on where you live, a handwritten (holographic) will may not be legally binding, although it is usually given some consideration. It's best to check the laws and consult a lawyer to avoid any regrettable mistakes."

GP: "You're right. It's a bit like doing a major repair job on your car without consulting the vehicle's manual or a qualified mechanic—better to trust a professional than risk a faulty job."

Charles: "Right. A holographic will is a temporary fix until you can get a formal one, which is generally more acceptable."

GP: "At death, a taxpayer is deemed to have disposed of all assets at fair market value unless the property is transferred to a spouse or a spousal trust."

Charles: "If you don't have a spouse, then you need to consider how the taxes will be paid so you don't leave your loved ones with debt. Filing taxes at death is a must, including a final return and sometimes a trust return. A clearance certificate is crucial to close the tax file without issues."

GP: "I don't like taxes, but I'd hate for my family to deal with that. More planning is needed to ensure my Money stays with them."

Charles: "Probate is the court process that confirms a will's validity and can be costly. Assigning direct beneficiaries for assets can avoid these fees."

GP: "More fees on top of taxes that my loved ones need to worry about."

Charles: "Check out this cheat sheet, GP.

- Who will be my beneficiaries and why?
- How much is needed to provide for my dependents?
- If I have assets I wish to transfer before I die, I should seek advice on potential capital gains.
- Always add a named beneficiary to my investment accounts to bypass the will and any probate costs.
- Beneficiary designations outside of the will remain confidential.
- Consider joint title with rights of survivorship for asset ownership when possible.
- Buying life insurance can create an asset, instantly providing for loved ones or leaving a legacy for my family or a charity.
- Life insurance beneficiaries can receive lump-sum amounts or guaranteed payments for a set period—I decide what is best.

- Make a will and keep it updated.
- Consider debts to be paid at death and whether my estate will have the funds to pay them.
- The fewer assets that pass through the will, the better to avoid probate fees.
- Seek advice from an independent financial advisor, as well as a lawyer and an accountant."

GP: "Great checklist, Charles! But remember to embrace life's uncertainties. Not all stories follow a set pattern, and not all poems rhyme. It's okay not to have all the answers, we just need to know the right people to bring on our financial journey. No one know exactly what the future holds. Charles, I know you will be a guiding light on the highway of so many people's lives, helping them reach their destination."

Charles "Thank you GP for being my guiding light."

> **NUTS AND BOLTS**
>
> - Think about what you want to leave behind for your family and how to take care of them.
> - Talk to a financial advisor to help you plan.
> - Decide on what you want for the end of your life and tell your advisor and lawyer.
> - Make time to see your lawyer to write a will and get advice specifically for you.
>
> This is your Money, and your family's future. It is in your hands!
>
> Make sure you do it right for the ones you love.

**May your actions lead you to your dreams.
Everything is possible!**

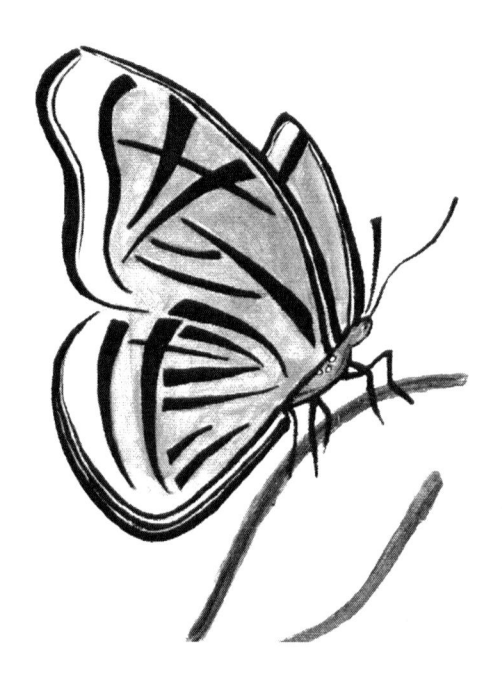

## The Desire to Change

To those who have Dreams and are willing to:

- Set GOALS to achieve them
- Create a vision PLAN
- Learn DISCIPLINE and WILL POWER
- Practice to PERFECT
- Persist to WIN

# YOUR 30-DAY CHALLENGE
## TO KICK-START YOUR FINANCIAL JOURNEY

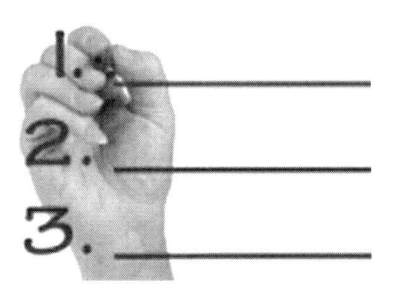

*"The best place to start is where you are with what you have."*
—CHARLES SCHWAB

**Starting** is the most important task.

Embrace our 30-Day Plan to pave the way to success. This isn't just a theoretical exercise; it's a practical approach to forming beneficial financial habits. With insights from *Who Took My Money?* recognize how debt hampers your well-being and take decisive steps to improve your financial health. Act now by applying these principles. Download the essential worksheets from whotookmymoney.ca and allocate time to implement this plan. Witnessing your financial transformation will assure you there's no reason to revert to old habits.

After facing financial challenges, the motivation to change and develop new, healthier financial behaviors becomes apparent. It requires courage and commitment to make these changes last.

### MY FINANCIAL WELL-BEING
1. I will save consistently, assess, and adjust my budget to improve financial satisfaction.

2. I will enhance my spending habits and focus on essential purchases by tracking my daily expenses in my journal.

3. I will plan my financial journey, setting clear short-term and long-term goals.

4. Recognizing that Money is a tool for achieving goals, I will make financial choices that reflect my values.

5. I am committed to living debt-free, increasing savings, and achieving financial freedom to enhance my life and support my loved ones.

6. A positive mindset and adaptability are crucial to following and adjusting my financial plan.

7. I seek financial stability to maintain peace of mind and ensure a future without financial stress.

8. This year, thanks to my new financial management plan, I will

   - Reduce my debt by_____.
   - Build my emergency fund to_____.
   - Deposit_____in my savings and_____in my investment accounts.

I own my future and will approach financial management with enthusiasm.

## KEEPING A FINANCIAL JOURNAL

Every time you spend Money, you should note down *what* you spent, *why* you spent it, *whether* it was a planned or an impromptu purchase, and the emotions you experienced at that time. It's important to acknowledge your feelings about embarking on this program, whether it be enthusiasm, apprehension, frustration, regret, or hope. Track the changes you make to support your financial fitness goals and observe when you fall back into old spending patterns.

Whether your journal is digital or on paper is up to you; the key is to be honest and not worry about grammar or coherence. This financial journal is an essential tool in your quest to become more financially aware and assert control over your Money, preventing it from controlling you.

| TODAY, WHAT HAPPENED WITH MY MONEY? |                          |
|-------------------------------------|--------------------------|
| I have earned                       | _____.         |
| My spending was                     | _____.         |
| I have spent on                     | _____.         |
| Net remaining:                      | _____.         |
| It made me happy:                   | YES or NO                |

Based on our own experience, we believe that keeping a daily financial journal is instrumental to achieving financial goals. A journal is also particularly helpful for managing emotional spending and beneficial for everyone committed to financial improvement.

## INVOLVING THE FAMILY IN FINANCES

Together, we achieve more. You can initiate meaningful financial discussions with your family today, as collective involvement is key to success. Together, you can get creative and assemble a piggy bank using materials you have without additional spending. Embracing values like honesty, love, and courage, you can be confident in your family's ability to help you reach your financial goals.

This streamlined version removes repetition and focuses on clear action steps, maintaining the original message's spirit and intent.

Money management is like learning a new sport or any skill—your ability improves over time. Remember to enjoy the journey and keep the process fun and engaging!

- Track your progress through the 30-day plan.
- Find forums for sharing success stories, asking questions, and community support. visit whotookmymoney.ca

## 30-DAY FINANCIAL TRANSFORMATION PLAN
### Preparation

- Read *Who Took My Money?* for insight into personal financial habits.
- Commit to tracking all expenses and improving spending behavior.
- Set clear financial goals and maintain self-accountability.
- Download financial worksheets from whotookmymoney.ca.

## WEEK 1: ESTABLISHING A STRONG FOUNDATION

- Day 1: start a financial journal to document spending and emotional insights.
- Use only cash for all purchases to better feel the impact of spending.
- Create a dream board for motivation.
- Take a "snapshot" of your net worth to assess your financial status.
- Draft a budget, prioritizing savings and necessary expenses.
- Organize financial documents daily and initiate a debt elimination plan.

**WEEK 2: BUILDING AWARENESS AND MAKING ADJUSTMENTS**

- Daily: reflect on your financial journal to identify spending triggers.
- Adjust budget allocations based on insights from your spending journal.
- Read *The Wealthy Barber* for further financial guidance.
- Reallocate funds between budget categories as life happens.
- Complete any unfinished tasks from week 1.

**WEEK 3: GAINING CONTROL AND PROTECTING ASSETS**

- Daily: continue the cash-only discipline and update your financial journal.
- Ensure legal documents such as your will are up to date.
- Review and adjust insurance policies.
- Use the "Tax Man" worksheet to prepare for tax season.

**WEEK 4: REINFORCING GOOD HABITS AND CELEBRATING PROGRESS**

- Daily: document spending and adjust your budget in real-time.
- Compare actual spending to your budget plan.
- Adjust your financial routine based on monthly insights.
- Reflect on the alignment of financial choices with personal values.
- Set yourself up for success by staying within your budget.

**ONGOING COMMITMENT**

- Maintain the daily financial journal to track your spending.
- Manage cash flow, review budget allocations and file receipts weekly.
- Review and adjust the budget monthly, reassess debt strategies and plan investments.

## EMBRACING THE FINANCIAL JOURNEY

- Recognize the importance of consistent financial planning.
- Educate yourself continuously on financial management.
- Celebrate each step of progress and stay resilient against challenges.
- Make financial planning an enjoyable and integral part of life.

By diligently following this 30-day guide with dedication, you'll work towards financial independence, build sustainable habits, and involve your family in creating a secure financial future.

# GP'S EASY TIPS FOR FINANCIAL MANAGEMENT

- **Freeze credit card use.** Freeze your credit cards in a block of ice to prevent impulsive spending. As the ice takes time to melt, you'll have the opportunity to reconsider your purchases.
- **Cash-only for small expenses.** Allocate a specific daily budget for minor expenses and use cash only. Physically fold each bill in half and organize them in your wallet to monitor spending.
- **Try smart spending over deprivation.** Prioritize value-driven spending decisions instead of cutting back on everything.
- **Review financial goals.** Regularly reassess your financial goals, including timelines, allocations, and priorities, to ensure they reflect your current aspirations. Understand that priorities may evolve with active financial engagement.
- **Educate yourself on Investments.** Investigate various investment opportunities through reading newspapers, online exploration, and professional consultations. Determine which options, like rental real estate or dividend stocks, align with your financial objectives.
- **Celebrate** your financial discipline by rewarding yourself for reaching milestones. This practice is enjoyable and reinforces the benefits of hard work.
- **Be consistent with your financial plan.** Commit to daily reviews and monthly modifications of your financial plan. This includes managing debts to build towards financial freedom.
- **Engage** in routine financial reviews each day to maintain clarity and streamline end-of-month accounting.
- **Be resilient.** If you stray from your budget or savings plan, acknowledge the slip, understand why it happened, and get

back on track by revisiting the fundamental strategies you set up initially.
- **Make informed decisions** about how to invest your savings. Don't shy away from consulting financial experts to navigate your path toward financial security.
- **Keep expanding your financial literacy** by reading reputable books on the subject.

## REFLECTIONS ON WEALTH AND LIFE

GP: "Money's journey mirrors our own. A long time ago, money transactions were done through bartering. Today, we are far from exchanging a chicken for an animal skin ! Financial transactions can be done virtually. Yet, its fundamental role endures. It's not the accumulation of wealth but what we do with it that forges legacies. Integrity, perseverance, and informed decisions allow great opportunities."

Charles: "Wisely spoken, GP! Let us honor Money as a reliable ally, stewarding it with care to sculpt a future replete with prosperity and light."

GP: "And yet, Charles, life is unpredictable. Like Forest Gump said: "Life is like a box of chocolates. You never know what you're going to get." So, let's be prepared as much as we can for any unforeseen situation. Most importantly, never lose faith in our ability to drive through rough roads!"

Charles: "It reminds me of mother's musings: 'Convey your deepest desires to a butterfly, for in their silent flight, your wishes will find a voice.' She believed in the ritual of setting free our dreams with these delicate messengers, entrusting them to the heavens, lending our aspirations the wings to ascend."

GP: "Your mother loves butterflies for they represent freedom and gentleness. Their wings are a symbol of love and joy."

The best way to learn is to play use multiple financial mind games and tools to increase your financial literacy and success.

"You have succeeded in life when all you really want is only what you really need."

~Vernon Howard

Visit whotookmymoney.ca for additional information on personal finances and various calculation tools.

# ADDITIONAL READING

*The Richest Man in Babylon* by George S. Clason

*Think and Grow Rich* by Napoleon Hill

*The Soul of Money* by Lynne Twist

*The Path to Happiness and Wealth* by Steve Rhode

*Lessons in Mastery* by Anthony Robbins

*Start Late, Finish Rich* by David Bach

*The Wealthy Barber* by David Chilton

*The Life, Lessons & Rules for Success* by influential individuals

*The Millionaire Next Door* by Thomas J. Stanley and William D. Danko

*The Total Makeover Workbook* by Dave Ramsey

*Warren Buffet 43 Lessons for Business & Life* by Keith Lard

# BIBLIOGRAPHY

Board of Governors of the Federal Reserve System. "Report on the Economic Well-Being of US Households in 2018." May 2019. https://www.federalreserve.gov/publications/files/2018-report-economic-well-being-us-households-201905.pdf.

El Issa, Erin. "2023 American Household Credit Card Debt Study." NerdWallet. January 8, 2024. https://www.nerdwallet.com/article/credit-cards/average-credit-card-debt-household.

Federal Reserve Bank Of New York. "Center for Microeconomic Data." Last modified October 31, 2023. https://www.newyorkfed.org/microeconomics/hhdc.html.

Ritchie, Sarah. "Almost Half of Canadians Living Paycheque to Paycheque as Conservative Support Grows: Poll." *The Globe and Mail*. Last modified September 2, 2023. https://www.theglobeandmail.com/canada/article-almost-half-of-canadians-living-paycheque-to-paycheque-as-tory-support/.

# RESOURCES

Good savings on income tax and more
Taxtips.ca (Canada)—irs.gov (US)

Trans Union Credit Bureau
transunion.ca/

Latest bankruptcy statistics
www.bankruptcyaction.com

### ONLINE COURSES, ACADEMIC JOURNAL AND WEBSITES

**Investopedia**—Provides a wealth of articles, tutorials, and explainers on every aspect of finance and investing.

**National Endowment for Financial Education (NEFE)** - Offers a variety of educational programs designed to help individuals at all levels of financial literacy improve their understanding of financial principles and practices.

**Journal of Financial Planning**—Contains research and advice on a variety of topics relevant to financial planners, including investment strategies, retirement planning, and tax advice.

**SolutionFinance (Personal Finance)**—Offers several workshops on many aspects of personal finance.

**Planet Money by NPR**—Makes complex economic stories accessible and interesting, with insights that can apply to personal finance.

**Jump$tart National Educator Conference**—Focuses on educators who teach K-12 students about personal finance.

# DEAR READER

Start Your Engine on a Journey to Success.

It's time to slide into the driver's seat of your life. This book will rev up your knowledge, steering you through the twists and turns of financial wisdom.

Once you feel the thrill of the ride, share your story. Your insights from this journey could be the roadmap that guides others else to find their own path to success.

Think of this book as your personal GPS for navigating the roads to wealth and happiness. It's time to accelerate change, gear up for progress, and cruise towards the life you've always wanted.

Together, we're on this road trip to a better world. Buckle up, and let's embark on this adventure with the wind of change at our backs and a horizon of dreams ahead.

**A Personal Touch:** To further tailor this experience to your individual needs, we're offering a complimentary coaching session. As your Wealth Builder Coach, we are here to personalize the teachings of GP's principles, ensuring they align seamlessly with your unique financial circumstances.

Reach out to us.

Monique: info@moniquegagne.com

Cathie: info@moneyadvisors.ca

For your convenience and in addition to the book,

whotookmymoney.ca offers free access to calculation tools and other relevant information.

# UNDERSTANDING FINANCIAL TERMS

**Accrued interest** accumulates over time on a debt that you owe.

**Annual percentage rate** is the yearly cost of a loan expressed as a percentage. It includes interest and other charges, providing a comprehensive measure for comparing different credit offers. This rate is made transparent to consumers through the Federal Truth in Lending Act, aiding in financial decision-making.

**Bankruptcy:** a legal procedure governed by federal law that helps consumers who have too much debt.

**Collection agency:** a business that collects past due debts for other businesses, as well as individuals. Most collection agencies get paid for their services by taking a percentage of what they collect for their clients.

**Collateral:** assets pledged as security for a secured debt. If you do not pay a debt that you have collateralized, the creditor can take the collateral.

**Credit agreement:** a contract between a borrower and a creditor that details the amount borrowed, the applicable interest rate, and all other terms of the credit agreement.

**Credit score:** a numerical summary of your credit history, reflecting the likelihood of your ability to repay debts. Lenders use it to evaluate your creditworthiness for future borrowing.

**Debt consolidation:** the process of taking out a larger loan to pay off one or smaller loans.

**Finance charge:** another term for the interest you pay a credit card company when you do not pay your card balance in full each month as well as the amount of interest you pay on your outstanding loan balance. The finance charge is expressed as a percentage.

**Grace period:** the time during which you can pay your account balance in full without incurring finance charges.

**Open-end credit agreement:** a credit agreement with no specific date by which you must pay the account balance in full, although you must make monthly minimum payments on the balance. Credit cards are a common example of open-ended credit.

**Periodic rate:** an interest rate that gets charged for each period, such as monthly or quarterly. The terms of the interest rate are spelled out in your credit agreement.

**Unsecured debt:** a debt for which no assets are pledged to guarantee payment. The most common type of unsecured debt is credit card debt. It is a way for you to get your finances back on track by repaying some of what you owe but bankruptcy should not be taken lightly as it will impact your credit in the future.

# ACKNOWLEDGMENTS

Great projects start with a dream put into action. Without the help and support of many talented people, *Who Took My Money* would never have seen the light of day. The list of the wonderful friends and family who made this book possible through their belief in us, encouragement, suggestions, and expertise are lengthy.

Monique and Cathie are grateful for their wonderful family.

To our dear parents, you have blessed us with love, guidance, and meaningful growing experiences. Our wonderful children, you have been our purpose in life. Watching each of you grow in wisdom and love has been our true *joie de vivre*.

To our dear husbands Raymond and Paul, thank you for your constant support and belief in us. You made it possible to achieve this dream.

To our precious grandchildren, and the ones to come, our love goes out to you. We sincerely believe in sharing our life experiences wisdom and knowledge. This is our legacy of love we are leaving you with.

To our family and friends, you each have contributed to our journey and life purpose. Your true friendship means the world to us.

Dear life, thank you for teaching us the true value of money. We never stop to learn.

Thank you to our clients. Being able to share a part of us and help empower you with financial tools has been a real joy.

# MONIQUE GAGNÉ, MONEY-MOM

MONIQUE GAGNÉ has inspired and empowered thousands families to navigate their financial landscapes. She transitioned from fashion design and IT to become a mortgage agent and financial coach and is the author of Who Took My Money?, first published in 2009. Over the past decade, she seen how quickly money can fly away, leaving dreams deferred and opportunities missed, affecting everyone purchasing their first home to high earners struggling to stay ahead of their expenses.

A sought-after financial speaker and media guest, Monique shares her money advice through "The Power of Financial Happiness" connecting with her audience in a unique, engaging, and educational manner. She has recently authored a children's book to help the next generation, financial literacy.

Dedicated to making a difference, Monique has organized numerous fundraising events. Her initiative, the "Bear Largest Hug," involving nineteen high schools in the Ottawa region, raised significant funds for cancer care. She serves on several educational advisory committees. Living in Ottawa, Canada, Monique enjoys spending time at her cottage surrounded with her family and friends.

With a heart committed to serving others, Monique is not just a record of past achievements but a prologue to the future chapters of influence she is yet to write, continuing to embrace the world with wisdom, love, and financial enlightenment. Monique 's has many little secrets hidden under the hood and believe 'Money has wings'.

# CATHIE ORFALI, EPC, CFP, CEA, MFA-P

CATHIE ORFALI kick started her own financial plan at an early age when she made her first big investment buying her first home at the age of nineteen. Her career in finance spans several decades and in 2005 she founded her own financial services company Money Advisors. She was driven by a desire to get ahead and pay if forward. She knows that creating a successful financial plan can only be achieved when financial goals intertwine with a strong sense of one's life purpose, whether it is looking after one's family, running a great business or giving back to charity. One of her favorite questions is what do you want your legacy to be?

Cathie is also an accomplished real estate investor with an extensive real estate portfolio in Canada and the US. Over the years she has been the recipient of several awards including the Queens Jubilee distinction for outstanding service to her community award and was a recipient of the Ottawa Vanier Leading Women.

Giving back is part of her DNA whether she is serving on boards, organizing community events for those in need or walking the streets of slums abroad serving those living in extreme poverty.

She is grateful to have the opportunity to share her wealth creation strategies and financial tools. Cathie hopes this book will help ignite the readers sense of financial possibilities and life purpose.

**"MONEY AS WINGS"**

Manufactured by Amazon.ca
Acheson, AB